BACTRIA

BACTRIA

THE HISTORY
OF A
FORGOTTEN EMPIRE

H. G. Rawlinson

WESTHOLME
Yardley

Frontispiece: The Khamba Baba Column at Besnagar, an ancient city near Vidisha, Madhya Pradesh, India. This stone column, also known as the Heliodorus Pillar, was erected c. 110 BC. One of its incriptions reads: "This Garuda-standard of Vasudeva, the God of Gods/was erected here by the devotee Heliodoros,/the son of Dion, a man of Taxila,/sent by the Great Greek King/Antialkidas, as ambassador to/King Kasiputra Bhagabhadra, the Savior/son of the princess from Benares, in the fourteenth year of his reign."

Originally published in 1912.
This edition ©2013 Westholme Publishing.

Westholme Publishing, LLC
904 Edgewood Road
Yardley, Pennsylvania 19067
Visit our Web site at www.westholmepublishing.com

First Printing September 2013
ISBN: 978-1-59416-186-5
Also available as an eBook.

Printed in the United States of America.

DEDICATED TO

JAMES ADAM, Litt.D.

स्मरणार्थम्

" If through the Bactrian Empire European ideas were trans-
mitted to the Far East, through that and similar channels
Asiatic ideas found their way to Europe."—DRAPER : *Intellectual
Development of Europe*, I. ii.

यथा नदीनां बहवोऽम्बुवेगाः समुद्रमेवाभिमुखा द्रवन्ति.

Gita, XI.

" In the profound obscurity which envelops the history of
Bactria, we must cull with care all that can throw the least light
upon it."—SCHLEGEL.

CONTENTS

APPENDICES

LIST OF ILLUSTRATIONS

PREFACE

I HAVE to express my obligations to many whose kindness has enabled me to obtain access to the materials necessary for the publication of this monograph. Some years ago, through the courtesy of Mr. F. W. Thomas, I was permitted to use the India Office Library. Mr. H. H. Lake, Superintending Engineer of the Gwalior State, has provided me with a drawing and other details of the famous Bactrian pillar at Besnagar. This drawing was copied for me by Lieutenant M. G. G. Campbell, R.E., who was also good enough to prepare the valuable maps which greatly enhance the utility of the book. I have also to acknowledge the generous aid of the authorities of Emmanuel College, Cambridge, in defraying the expenses of the original edition. Lastly, I am deeply indebted to Professor E. J. Rapson, Professor of Sanskrit in the University of Cambridge, for his unfailing interest and invaluable advice. Professor Rapson has been kind enough to read through the

proof-sheets of this edition, and to add many sug-
gestions and corrections.

I should, perhaps, add that as this work is intended
for the general reader, the tiresome diacritical marks
which are the fashion in Oriental works have been
omitted.

H. G. RAWLINSON.

Poona, 1912.

INTRODUCTION

THE object of this book is to investigate the history
of the great Iranian province which formed the
eastern portion of the Persian Empire, and which,
after the Macedonian invasion, became an independent Greek kingdom. The valiant Greeks who ruled
the country were afterwards driven over the Hindu-
Kush, where they maintained themselves for nearly a
century longer, finally succumbing to the tribes from
the north which had originally displaced them. Thus
it will be seen that the history of Bactria falls naturally
into four divisions. Passing over the mass of legend
which surrounds the earliest period, centred chiefly
round the figure of Zarathustra Spitama, we find
ourselves on more solid ground when we come to
deal with Bactria as a satrapy of the Persian Empire.
After the overthrow of Persia by Alexander we enter
upon the second phase in the history of the country
—its subjugation and settlement by the Macedonians.
The third period begins with the revolt of Diodotus in
250 B.C., when Bactria assumes the rôle of an inde-

pendent Greek kingdom, extending its sway not only
over Sogdiana to the north, but over a great portion
of the modern Afghanistan and the Panjab. The
closing chapter of the history of the Bactrian Greeks
commences with their evacuation of the country
north of the Hindu-Kush, when they made Sâgala
their capital, and ends with their final supersession
by the Kushan monarchs.

BIBLIOGRAPHY

REFERENCES IN CLASSICAL LITERATURE.—The history of early Iran is involved in the greatest obscurity, and we are able to glean very little trustworthy information about Bactria before the foundation of the Persian Empire. The legends of the Avesta and the later Persian literature (especially the *Shahnama* of Firdousi) are not meant for serious history; they merely preserve in a poetic garb half-forgotten traditions of a time when Bactria was a small, independent kingdom, struggling for existence against the "Turanian" nomads. The only outstanding personality is that of Zoroaster, and the references to him may be founded upon a substratum of fact. Ctesias, a Greek physician at the court of Artaxerxes Mnemon, is the earliest Western author who attempted to write a history of early Iran. His long residence in the country, and access to state archives, gave him a unique opportunity, which, unfortunately, he utterly misused. Without critical faculty, and, like most Greeks, quite oblivious of the necessity of studying the classical tongue of the land, he records any wild fables and improbable tales he happens to pick up.

His stories of Semiramis, his legends of Zoroaster and the Scythian expedition of Cyrus the Great, and a host of other gossiping tales, passed into later history, and are reproduced without question by later writers. Aristotle discovered his untrustworthiness; his opinion is confirmed by the inscriptions, Herodotus, and Jewish history. We only know of Ctesias through the abridgements of Photius, the Byzantine ecclesiastic. Berosus, the Chaldean priest who wrote a great history of Babylonia, Media, and Persian about the time of Alexander the Great, probably preserved a mass of information which would have thrown light on the early history of Bactria.

For the Persian Empire we have, of course, the excellent first-hand evidence of Herodotus, of whom it is unnecessary to speak here. Herodotus, alas! carries us down to the Battle of Mycale only, and from 479 to 330 B.C. there is a great gap in our knowledge of Eastern Iran. A few scattered notices in books like the *Bibliotheca* of Diodorus of Sicily, a contemporary of Julius Cæsar, is all that we hear of Bactria for over a century.

Two historians have collected minute details of Alexander's campaign in Bactria. Of these, incomparably the greater is Arrian, a brilliant and versatile member of the Imperial Civil Service under the Emperor Hadrian. Scholar, soldier, and philosopher, Arrian was well fitted for the great task he undertook. The *Anabasis* is based on the works of Ptolemy and Aristobulus, first-rate material, admirably employed.

That delightful book, *De Rebus Gestis Alexandri Magni*, of Quintus Curtius,[1] belongs to a different order of literature. It is a popular book on a great subject, and the author's own ignorance of technical details of geography and tactics is made worse by his rather indiscriminate use of his authorities. One of them, Cleitarchus, is suspected, on one occasion at least, of eking out history with a dash of romance. On the other hand, Curtius does not trust his authorities blindly;[2] he mentions at least one episode omitted by Arrian;[3] and on the question of the locality of Zariaspa, the mysterious Bactrian town about which there is so much disagreement, he is much the clearer of the two.[4]

For the history of the Bactrian kings from the revolt of Diodotus to their extinction, our only authority is Justin,[5] the author of a work entitled *Trogi Pompei Philippicarum Epitoma*, a "kind of anthology,"[6] as he calls it, of the "Philippic history" of Trogus, an historian of the reign of Augustus. The original work is now lost, but Justin preserves innumerable facts about the revolt of Parthia and Bactria, and the Bactrian rulers of India, which are of inestimable value. Justin has often been blamed for his

---

[1] Date uncertain. He probably lived in the reign of Claudius

[2] *E.g.*, *De Reb. Gest.*, IX. 11, 21.

[3] The massacre of the Branchiadæ, perhaps passed over out of shame by Arrian and his authorities.

[4] See ch. i., *sub fin.*, of the *De Reb. Gest. Alex. Mag.*

[5] About A.D. 500.

[6] "Velut florum corpusculum."

b

inaccuracy. "Trogus is a sad historian, or Justus a vile abridger," remarks an eighteenth-century translator; "but as we have the testimony of famous men in favour of Trogus, Justin will stand condemned." This is ungrateful. He wrote, as Adolf Holm remarks, "for a circulating library public," and not for scholars. After a quite disproportionate popularity in the Middle Ages, Justin has been almost forgotten, and until a few years ago was treated by the modern editor with very scant courtesy. The only recent edition is the admirable French one by Garnier Frères, with a useful introduction and notes.

Strabo's *Geography* is another valuable authority for the history of Bactria. This work is a veritable mine of information about the tribes of Central Asia and India, as far as was known in the writer's days. Incidentally, Strabo adds a great many remarks about the history of the countries he describes, and in the case of Bactria and Bactrian India these are all-important.

A great many references of more or less value to the study of this subject occur in a variety of authors, from Clement of Alexandria to Isidore of Seville and the Byzantine historians. A considerable number of these have been collected by J. W. McCrindle in his series of translations of references to the East in Greek and Latin writers (*Ancient India as described by Classical Authors*, five vols. London, 1896).

For the history of Menander, of which fragments

are preserved by Justin and Strabo, we have valuable
evidence in the Pali philosophical dialogue, *The
Questions of Milinda*, translated by Dr. Rhys Davids
(*Sacred Books of the East*, XXXV.-XXXVI.). The
question how far this work is a mere romance, written
like Xenophon's *Cyropædia*, "non ad historiæ fidem
sed ad effigiem justi imperii," is not yet satisfactorily
settled.

The Chinese writers who refer to the Scythian
tribes which overthrew the Bactrian Greeks can only
be consulted by the ordinary student in translations.
The questions arising from their statements have
been discussed in a number of articles from the pens
of MM. Chavannes, Specht, and Sylvain Lévi, and
Messrs. F. W. Thomas, Fleet, and V. A. Smith, in
the various Oriental journals. The most useful books
dealing with this particular subject are probably
Deguigne's *Recherches sur quelques Evènements qui
concernent l'Histoire des Rois Grecs de la Bactriane*
(Mém. de l'Acad. des Inscrip. xxv.) and Dr. Otto
Franke's *Beiträge aus Chinesischen Quellen zur Kenntnis
der Turkovölker und Skythen Zentralasiens* (Berlin,
1904). The standard English translation of the
records of the Chinese pilgrims, from Fa-Hian
(A.D. 400) to Hiuen Tsiang (A.D. 629), is Beal's
Buddhist Records of the Western World, in Trübner's
Oriental Series. Hiuen Tsiang has recently been
retranslated by Watters (Oriental Translation Fund,
R.A.S., vols. xiv., xv.).

MODERN AUTHORITIES.—These may be divided into three classes: (a) History of Bactria and the surrounding countries; (b) Numismatics; (c) Books dealing with Græco-Indian art and the problem of the possibility of the influence of Greek culture upon India.

History of Bactria.—The earliest attempt to elucidate the history of the Indo-Greeks was made by Bayer, in a book published in St. Petersburg in 1798. Another early work was that of Thomas Maurice (1802), entitled *The Modern History of Hindoostan, comprehending that of the Greek Empire of Bactria, and Other Great Asiatic Kingdoms bordering on its Western Frontier.* But the first really scientific contribution to the history of this part of the world is Horace Hayman Wilson's magnificent *Ariana Antiqua* (1841), a monumental work of the highest value. Lassen's *Indische Alterthums-kunde*, and Spiegel's *Eranische Alterthümer* (Leipsic, 1878), are still useful upon many points. For the history of Parthia, Rawlinson's *Sixth Oriental Monarchy* remains an authoritative work. Professor von Gutschmidt, of Tübingen, has dealt at length with Bactrian problems in his contribution to the ninth edition of the *Encyclopædia Britannica* (*s.v.* "Persia," § 2). His *Geschichte Irans* (1888) is a serviceable book, "abounding in brilliant, if over-bold conjectures," as a recent critic observes. The principal works dealing with Syria and the Seleucids are M. Babelon's *Rois de Syrie*, and the admirable *House of Seleucus* of Mr. E. R.

Bevan. Mr. V. A. Smith, in his recent book, *The Early History of India* (Oxford, 1904), deals briefly but thoroughly with the whole question.[1]

Numismatics.—The history of the Bactrio-Greeks depends very largely upon coins, which link together the gaps between the scattered notices found in the classical writers. The magnificent coinage of the Bactrian Empire shows that the Greek conquerors must have been a people of high culture, and not the small settlement of semi-civilized veterans they are sometimes represented as being. These coins have been unearthed in great numbers, a fact in itself conclusively proving the prosperity of the Greeks in India. Many of them were struck by kings who are otherwise unknown to history, and a great deal of ingenuity has been displayed in the endeavour to arrange them in their proper chronological order.

The older discoveries of Wilson and Van Prinsep[2] are now embodied in more recent works. The chief book bearing on Bactrian numismatics is Gardner's *Catalogue of the Coins of Greek and Scythic Kings of Bactria aud India in the British Museum.* The same author has also issued a catalogue of the coins of the Seleucid kings, while Mr. Warwick Wroth deals with those of the Parthians. All these works contain

[1] The eleventh edition of the *Encyclopædia Britannica* contains an article on "Bactria" from the pen of Dr. Ed. Meyer. No new information, however, is given. It has a useful bibliography.

[2] Prinsep was the pioneer in Bactrian numismatics. The work he did in this subject was heroic.

valuable introductory remarks. For the Indian collections, we have numerous articles by General Sir A. Cunningham in the *Numismatic Chronicle*, and the valuable *Catalogue of Coins in the Calcutta Museum*, by Mr. V. A. Smith. Dr. Aurel Stein has written a useful pamphlet on *Zoroastrian Deities on Indo-Scythian Coins*, and Professor Rapson has contributed a very valuable résumé of his researches on Græco-Bactrian coins to the *Grundriss der Indo-arischen Philologie*, which is practically the last word on the subject. Von Sallet's *Die Nachfolger Alexanders des Grossen in Baktrien* (Berlin, 1878) will not, of course, be overlooked.[1]

Indo-Greek Art and Greek Influence on India.—The vexed question of Greek influence on India has received a good deal of attention in recent years. The exaggerated views of Weber and Niese have provoked a not unnatural reaction. Mr. V. A. Smith goes even so far as to say that Niese's "astonishing paradox" is "not supported by a single fact." Among the noteworthy contributions to the subject is W. W. Tarn's "Notes on Hellenism in Bactria and India" in the *Journal of Hellenic Studies*, 1902.[2] From the purely literary point of view, the fullest and most unbiassed discussion will be found in the concluding chapter of Professor Macdonell's *History of Sanskrit*

[1] See also Rapson's *Catalogue of the Coins of the Andhras* and the *Corolla Numismatica* (Oxford, 1906).

[2] See also the impartial summary in the relevant portions of the article on "Hellenism" in the *Encyclopædia Britannica*, eleventh edition.

Literature, with a copious bibliography of the subject at the end of the book. The Gandhara sculptures have been investigated by M. Foucher under the auspices of the Académie des Inscriptions et Belles Lettres ; the results may be seen in his *Notes sur la Géographie Ancienne du Gandhara, sur la Frontière Indo-Afghane*, and his more recent *L'art du Gandhara.* Mr. V. A. Smith's views were stated in his paper on "Græco-Roman Influence on the Civilization of Ancient India" (*J.A.S.B.*, 1889, p. 115).[1] From the Indian point of view, Mr. Havell, in his *Indian Sculpture and Painting* (1908), repudiates with vigour the suggestion that Indian art owes anything to the West. For foreign elements in Indian architecture, besides Cunningham's remarks in vol. v. of the *Archæological Survey of India*, the reader may refer to an article by W. Simpson, in the *Journal of the Institution of British Architects*, vol. i., p. 93.

[1] Mr. V. A. Smith has now set forth his views (greatly modified by recent criticism) in his *History of Fine Art in India and Ceylon* (Clarendon Press, 1911), chapter xi.

BACTRIA

CHAPTER I

GEOGRAPHY AND EARLY HISTORY OF BACTRIA

" Bâkhdhîm çrîrãm eredhvô drafshãm " (Bactra the beautiful, crowned with banners).—*Vend.*, I. 7.

THE name of Bactria, or Bactriana,[1] was given by classical writers to the vast tract of country which lies between the Hindu-Kush and the Oxus. On its southern and eastern flanks the great mountain barrier divides it from Thibet and India; on its western side lie the great Carmanian desert, and the grassy downs of Aria and Margiana.[2] Beyond the Oxus

[1] The Greek " Bactria" comes from the Persian *Bâkhtri* of the cuneiform inscriptions. The earlier form, found in the Zend Avesta, is *Bâkhdhi*. In Pehlevi this became *Bâkhal*, or *Bâkhli*, by a common metathesis of "dh" and "l," whence the modern (Mahommedan) *Balkh*. The Greeks naturally adopted the West Persian form, in use (as the Behistun Inscr., col. i. 6, shows) among the people they came in contact with. The old derivation of Bactria, from *A-paktra*, "northern" (Bactria being the most northerly Arian settlement), is plausible, but unsound.

[2] The modern Herat and Merv, both Iranian settlements of great antiquity. Margiana (*Margush*, Behist. Inscr., III. 3) was counted as part of Bactria by the Persians for adminis-

1

to the north stretches the little-known and sparsely
inhabited region of Sogdiana, as far as the Jaxartes ;
beyond that, again, lie the limitless steppes of Central
Asia, inhabited by the vast hordes of nomadic
Scythians, whose presence on the borders of their
territories constituted a perpetual menace to the
Iranian population of the fertile valleys.

Bactria was noted for its fertility. It is called by
Strabo " the pride of Ariana,"[1] and in later days it
paid the large sum of 360 talents tribute to the
Persian revenues. It was well watered. Besides the
mighty Oxus, the Arius (the modern Hari-rud), and
several less important streams, irrigate the country.
It produced all the Greek products except the olive ;
and silphium, which was useful as an article of
commerce, as well as for fattening an excellent breed
of sheep, grew in great quantities on the slopes of
the Hindu-Kush.[2] Lucerne, the " Medica herba,"
as it was called from the place of its origin, grew
freely in Bactria, and produced admirable fodder for
the famous Bactrian horses, helping, perhaps, partially

---

trative purposes. Μαργιανή, like Βακτριανή, is an adjective, γῆ
being understood. It means the land of the Μάργος, river
(modern Murgab).

[1] πρόσχημα τῆς 'Αριανῆς, XI. 11, 1.   So Vergil :

> " Sed neque Medorum silvæ ditissima terra
> Laudibus Italiæ certet, non Bactra neque Indi."
> > *Georg.*, II. 137.

[2] Strabo, *ibid.* Silphium (assafœtida) was looked upon by
the ancient Greeks as a condiment. It was also used medicin-
ally. It is difficult to understand their addiction for what we
should consider a nauseating substance. It is still so used in
parts of India, however. See also Arrian, *Anab.*, III. 29.

to account for the reputation which the Bactrian cavalry acquired.[1] The well-known description of Bactrian fertility by Quintus Curtius has been praised by subsequent travellers. " The soil of Bactria," he tells us, " varies considerably in its nature. In some spots extensive orchards and vineyards produce abundant fruit of a most delicious quality. The soil there is rich and well-watered. The warmer parts produce crops of corn ; the rest is better for pasture-land. The fertile portion is densely populated, and rears an incredible number of horses."[2] It is inter-esting to compare what is told us by ancient writers with the remarks of a recent visitor to these regions. It will be seen that the agricultural features of the country have altered little ; incidentally, the similarity between the two descriptions testifies to the accuracy of the classical geographers.

The *Times* correspondent with Lumsden's force, writing on March 12, 1882, describes the country as

---

[1] It is curious that so little is said about the (afterwards) famous Bactrian *camels*. They must have been extensively used on the trade routes. The Parthians employed them as ammunition animals, to carry fresh supplies of arrows for their mounted infantry. But they are never mentioned among the products of Bactria by classical writers, and only figure once on the coins.

[2] " Bactriæ terra multiplex et varia natura est. Alibi multa arbor, et vitis largos mitesque fructus alit ; solum pingue crebri fontes rigant ; quæ mitiora sunt frumento conseruntur ; cetera armentorum pabulo cedunt," etc. A recent traveller remarks : " The language of the most graphic writer could not delineate the country with greater exactness " (Sir A. Burnes, *Journey to Bokhara*, i. 245). The various passages are quoted in Appendix V., pp. 162-166.

follows: "The south branch of the Parapamisus is
represented by gentle undulations of gravelly soil,
covered with camel thorn and assafœtida, which
intervene between Herat and the frontier. . . . Groves
of pistachio and mulberry trees, bushes, wild carrots,
testify to the richness of the soil, irrigated in many
places by streams of purest water alive with fish."
The extraordinary fertility here referred to extends,
however, only over the central part of the country—
the alluvial lands watered by the Oxus and Arius.
All along the western frontier lay great shifting sand-
dunes, forming an almost impenetrable barrier to
invaders, as Alexander found. Curtius tells us that
after a north-west gale it is not uncommon for the
whole face of the country to be altered, roads being
blotted out, landmarks obliterated, and fresh sand-
hills piled up, so that the traveller can only guide
himself by the stars. As Strabo and Arrian remark,[1]
this has a curious effect on the rivers. Unable to
maintain their course, they are gradually absorbed
in the overwhelming mass of shifting sands and
disappear. The Arius in this way comes to an end
in the Tejend oasis, being unable to cut a channel
in the shifting Turcoman deserts; and even the
lordly Oxus suffers in the same manner. Matthew
Arnold graphically describes the difficulties which
beset the stream on its course to the Aral Sea,[2] in
language which would apply with equal truth to the
other Bactrian rivers:

---

[1] *Geog.*, XI. 5; *Anab.*, IV. 6. *Vide* the passage (*g*), on
p. 165.
[2] Its present course, not the ancient one.

"Then sands begin
To hem his watery course, and dam his streams,
And split his currents, that for many a league
The shorn and parcelled Oxus strains along
Through beds of sand and matted rushy isles."

The same fate probably overtook the Sogd, or Polytimetus,[1] in Sogdiana, which, according to Curtius, "plunges into the bowels of the earth," and is lost to sight.[2] Sogdiana, the little-known land north of Bactria, was not so fertile or so thickly populated. From the Oxus to the Jaxartes lay a succession of rolling steppes, interspersed with patches of barren desert. Only round Maracanda and on the river-banks was any attempt made at cultivation. The inhabitants were scattered and few in number; probably dread of the nomads from across the river, as well as the nature of the country itself, made agriculture hardly worth while.

The courses of the rivers, and indeed the general climatic conditions of this part of Asia, appear to have changed a good deal since the days of the Macedonian invasion. The same has happened in the Panjab and in Khotan; the latter country, now a barren waste, was once a fertile land with cities and orchards,

[1] *Vide* note, p. 17.

[2] Quintus Curtius, VII. 10, 1. Curtius says the Polytimetus plunges into a narrow gorge and then disappears. He states that the roaring of the water may be heard for some distance underground, and the course of the streams traced by the sound. Modern travellers do not confirm this story. Perhaps he is thinking of the *kanats*, or underground watercourses, still a feature of the country (Ἐπίνομοι). The passage is quoted in the Appendix, p. 166.

as recent explorations have revealed. The bare plains of the Mekran cannot have been as utterly destitute of water and forage as they are now, or Alexander could hardly, even with the losses he sustained, have crossed those terrible deserts at all. Perhaps the monsoon current, which now deflects abruptly to the east off the Bombay coast, once penetrated northwards as far as Karachi. The courses of the "five rivers" of the Panjab have altered considerably since the third century B.C.; the Oxus, again, which in Strabo's day emptied itself into the Caspian Sea near Krasnovodsk, now flows into the Aral Sea. The modern town of Balkh is some miles distant from the river (the ancient Bactrus), on the banks of which it originally stood.

One of the most characteristic features of Bactria and Sogdiana was the succession of great natural forts scattered over the face of the country, reminding the traveller of similar strongholds, so common in the Bombay Deccan, which played such a prominent part in Maratha history. Like the Maráthas, the Iranians of Bactria had recognized their strategic value, and in many cases had made them almost impregnable. The successive reduction of these forts taxed all the resources of Alexander himself. Strabo gives us a minute account of these great strongholds.[1] The chief of them was the citadel of Sisimithres, surrendered by Oxyartes to Alexander. It is stated to have been fifteen stadia high, and eighty stadia in circumference at the base. The summit formed a

[1] XI., 88, 4, etc. See the passage quoted in Appendix V., pp. 164-165 (f).

broad plateau, capable, when properly provisioned and supplied with water, of supporting a garrison of 500 men for an indefinite period; it even had cultivated fields at the top, and was more like a town than a fortress. Maracanda, the capital of the province of Sogdiana, was more than double this in height; and we hear of another strong fortress which was held against the Macedonians by the Iranian prince Arimazes. So confident were the defenders of their security that they rejected Alexander's overtures with scorn, declaring that troops must be able to fly in order to scale their walls. Arimazes found out his mistake to his cost. Bactra, the capital of Bactria,[1] was also a city of great strength, though this was due to artificial rather than natural causes.[2] It resisted the forces of Antiochus the Great, and compelled him to raise the siege and acknowledge the independence of the country. It is probably to this great achievement that Polybius refers,[3] when he speaks of the "siege of Bactra," as one of the most renowned blockades in military history, and a synonym for stubborn resistance.

Bactra was celebrated in Iranian history for many associations. Hither, according to an ancient tradition,

[1] Other cities of which we hear are Cariatæ and Adraspa, or Darapsa.

[2] Diod., II. 6 : ἡ γὰρ Βακτριανὴ χώρα πολλαῖς καὶ μεγάλαις οἰκουμένη πόλεσι μίαν μὲν εἶχεν ἐπιφανεστάτην, ἐν ᾗ συνέβαινεν εἶναι τὰ βασίλεια. αὕτη δ' ἐκαλεῖτο μὲν Βάκτρα, μεγέθει δὲ καὶ τῇ κατὰ τὴν ἀκρόπολιν ὀχυρότητι πολὺ πασῶν διέφερε.

[3] Polybius, xxix. 12, 8. We cannot be certain of this, though von Gutschmidt takes it for granted. Polybius might possibly be thinking of the mythical siege by Semiramis.

came the prophet Zarathustra to expound the doctrines afterwards associated with his name. Here, too, stood one of the many rich temples of the goddess Anahid, or Anaitis—the Tanata of the Persians, and Anânita of the Avesta hymns. The shrines of this goddess were always a source of great wealth to the city in which they stood. At Ecbatana her temple had silver tiles and gilt[1] pillars ; equally wealthy was another at Elymais. On more than one occasion needy Syrian monarchs were constrained to plunder these opulent fanes to replenish their coffers.[2] The wealth and popularity of the temples of the goddess were partly due to the licentious nature of her rites. At Acilisene, in Armenia (in which country she was especially popular), girls prostituted themselves in her honour, and incidentally, no doubt, to the great enhancement of the temple revenues.[3]

Another festival of Anaitis, called the Sacæa, was also accompanied by wild and licentious revels, the celebrants, men and women, indulging in excesses which remind the student of similar orgies which accompanied the Hindu festival of the Sakti Puja, described by the Abbé Du Bois.[4] This took place at Zela, and the participants dressed in Scythian costume. The festival is said to have commemorated the victory of Cyrus over the Scythians ;[5] this explanation, though

---

[1] κεχευσωμένα (Polybius, X. 27, 12).

[2] Antiochus Epiphanes and Mithridates I. both did so (vide Maccabees, I. vi. 13, and II. i. 13).

[3] Strabo, XI. 14, 16.

[4] Mœurs, Institutions et Cérémonies des Peuples d'Inde (trans. Beauchamp, Clarendon Press), ii. 9.

[5] Strabo, XI., viii., §§ 4-6.

not itself correct, doubtless contains the germs of the truth. Anaitis was a Scythian goddess, and her cult was probably brought into Media by Cyrus on his return from the East. She was then identified, as Herodotus tells us, with the Assyrian Mylitta (the Arabian Alytta), the Venus Urania of Greece.[1]

One of her most celebrated shrines stood in Bactra, and probably antedated by many centuries the Iranian occupation of the city. Artaxerxes Mnemon, the victor at Cunaxa, was a special devotee of this goddess, who appears by this time to have become associated in some way with the Persian Mithra, perhaps as his feminine counterpart.[2] It was a sign of the degradation of the Persian creed, noted already by Herodotus, that its followers began to hanker after the anthropomorphic religion of their neighbours, forsaking the pure Unitarianism which so commended them to the Jews.[3] Artaxerxes was an especial offender, and one of his acts was to adorn the shrine at Bactra with a magnificent statue. This famous image is celebrated in the Avesta hymns,[4] where the Bactrian Anahid is described as the "High girdled one, clad in a mantle of gold, having on thy head a golden crown, with eight rays and a hundred

[1] Herod., I. 131. The identification is attributed to Artaxerxes Longimanus (not Mnemon, as Clement of Alexandria states, led away probably by the further honours paid to the goddess by the latter).

[2] Or *śakti*, to adopt the Indian term. The Bactrian Anahid was also, by the Iranians, looked upon as a *yazata*, or spirit, of the Ardvisura (Oxus), on whose banks the temple stood.

[3] Herod., *loc. cit.*: "The Persians do not think the gods have human forms. They sacrifice to sun, moon, fire, air, and the winds. . . . They have since learnt to sacrifice to . . . Mylitta, whom the Persians call Mithra" (*i.e.*, Anahid).

[4] *S.B.E.*, vol. ii., p. 82.

stars, and clad in a robe of thirty otter-skins of the sort
with shining fur." The opulence of the Bactrian goddess is in keeping with the wealth and splendour of her
other shrines. She figures, in her eight-rayed crown,
on a fine coin of the Græco-Bactrian Demetrius ;[1] and
Clement of Alexandria refers to a statue of Aphrodite
Tanais, (meaning, no doubt Tanata, the Persian name
for Anaitis,) existing in his days at Bactra. Such, then,
was Bactra, the capital of Eastern Iran. Her ancient
shrine, a place of pilgrimage to Scythian and Persian
alike, was very probably a source of great wealth and
renown; her associations with Zoroaster,[2] and her great
natural strength as a fortress, added to her celebrity;
and besides, situated as she was in the heart of Iran,
and on the high road to Europe and Eastern Asia on
the one hand, and China and India on the other, her
commercial and strategic importance would be hard
to overestimate. Unfortunately, this part of Asia is
practically unexplored as far as archæological research
is concerned ; modern travellers have failed to detect
any remains of its ancient glory in the modern Mahommedan town, though vague reports of the discovery of
inscribed bricks which occasionally appear may point
to the existence of cuneiform inscriptions. In any case,
in a town like Bactra, continually inhabited and rebuilt
by successive conquerors, any remains of the ancient
shrine of Anahid, or of the Greek occupation, must, if

---

[1] Gardner, *Catalogue of the Greek and Scythic Kings of Bactria
and India*, iii. 1. Perhaps also on a coin of Euthydemus in
H. H. Wilson's *Ariana Antiqua*, ii. 1 (Wilson says it is Apollo).

[2] We hear of a great fire temple—the Nas-bohâr, or Temple
of the Spring—in Firdousi. But this seems to have dated from
Sassanian times only.

they exist, lie buried under many yards of débris. The Iranians spoke with affectionate pride of "Bactra the beautiful," but it did not favourably impress the Macedonians when they occupied it. The clean and spacious suburbs won their admiration, but they were disgusted at the (to them) barbarous practice of exposing corpses to be devoured by birds, which is enjoined by Zoroastrianism. The swarms of half-savage pariah dogs which haunt the streets of Oriental cities were especially common in Bactra, the centre of the most conservative type of the ancient Iranian creed, as Zoroastrianism regards the dog as a sacred animal, to injure which is an offence computed in the Vendidâd as more heinous than manslaughter. The dog was originally protected by the precepts of Zarathustra, no doubt because of its useful scavenging habits, which made it in primitive times a valuable means of promoting sanitation. The custom of attaching a sacred character to useful animals in order to protect them may be illustrated from the case of the Hindus, who similarly revere the cow. Strabo, however, declares the Bactrians practised the savage habit, common among the Scythian tribes, of handing the old and infirm over to the dogs to devour. He asserts that these dogs were called "Entombers,"[1] and that the streets of the city were "full of bones" in consequence. This was certainly not originally an Iranian custom, though it must be mentioned that a persistent opinion prevailed among the Greeks that some Iranian tribes gave their dead to the dogs. In the *Clementine Recognitions* we find it recorded that

---

[1] ἐνταφιασταί. The passage is given in full in Appendix V. *e*), p. 164, *q.v.*

one of the effects of the preaching of St. Thomas was
that "very few of the Medes now give their dead to
the dogs."[1] An ancient custom, still practised by the
Parsis, was to show the corpse to a dog (to drive off
the fiends), before giving it over to the vultures at the
dakhma, or Tower of Silence. Strabo may be referring
to some garbled account of this custom (which was
put down by Alexander as a detestable habit), or he
may be referring to an actual practice among the
Scythian populace of Bactra; such customs were
common north of the Oxus, as the Scythians had
a prejudice against letting their older people die
naturally. The Caspii starved them to death;[2] the
Massagetæ are said to have devoured them![3] A
similar custom is recorded of the island of Ceos.[4]

There seems to be very little doubt that the
population of Bactria was largely Scythian. The
"Turanian"[5] tribes who dwelt all along the north
of the Iranian settlements of Western and Central
Asia, known indifferently to classical writers as Sacæ,
or Scythians, had occupied the fertile plains of the
Oxus long before the advent of the Aryans. "The
Bactrian Empire was founded by the Scythians,"
says Justin;[6] and Strabo tells us that this event
occurred at the same time that these nomads occupied
the fertile valleys, afterwards known as Sacastené.[7]

[1] Second or third century A.D. IX. 29: "Nec multi apud
Medos canibus objiciunt mortuos."

[2] Strabo, *Geog.*, XI. 11, 8.   [3] *Ibid.*, XI. 8, 6.

[4] *Ibid.*, X. 5, 6.   [5] *I.e.*, non-Iranian.

[6] Justin, II. 1.

[7] *Geog.*, XI. 8, 4. Sacastené = Saka-stan, the land where
the Sakas settled (*cf.* Afghanistan, Hindustan, etc.). The word
first occurs, I believe, in Isidore of Seville.

We may, in a word, conjecture that Bactria underwent the same change that we can so clearly trace in Armenia. Armenia, when it becomes first known to history, is clearly Turanian. Its inscriptions, language, religion, all point to this. Then, about the seventh century B.C., a change comes over the face of the country. Herodotus writes of Armenia in his day as populated by an Aryan race, akin to the Phrygians. In Bactria, as in Armenia, "everything seems to indicate that a strange people had immigrated into the land, bringing with them a new language, new manners and customs, and a new religious system."[1] We see, however, numerous traces in Bactria of the old order of things. We have already referred to the worship of Anahid, with her Sacæan ritual, celebrated by priests in Scythian vestments; the very fact that her statue in Bactra was "clothed in otter-skins" seems to show that she came from the frozen steppes beyond the Jaxartes.[2] Other barbarous customs, referred to on a previous page, appear to be undoubtedly of Scythian origin. Strabo says the custom of doing away with the dead and infirm obtaining in Bactria is practically identical with that of the Scythians.[3]

The Iranians who conquered Bactria did not, of course, oust or exterminate the primitive inhabitants. Their numbers were too few, and the country too vast. Apparently, they merely seized and fortified

[1] Rawlinson, *Sixth Oriental Monarchy*, ch. ix.

[2] It is significant that she is a favourite goddess of the Kushan kings, who were Scythians. The name NANO appears on the coins of Huvishka and others.

[3] *Geog.*, XI. 1, 3.

the great natural strongholds with which the country abounded, and dwelt there in peace and safety. They appear to have agreed excellently with the aboriginal inhabitants. Their rule was probably easy, and imposed nothing more than a light tribute in kind upon the rude cultivators. The most probable supposition is that the pure Iranian nobles formed a kind of "equestrian order,"[1]—mounted knights who could quell without difficulty the ill-armed and ill-disciplined pedestrian population of the country. We find confirmation for this theory in what is told us about the rude Bactrian infantry, armed with "Medic turbans, bows of Bactrian cane, and short spears," who accompanied Xerxes.[2] These are obviously not the picked regiments left behind with Mardonius on account of their efficiency. Quintus Curtius, too, refers to a "body of 7,000 Bactrian equites whom the rest obeyed";[3] these are, no doubt, the Iranian ruling caste. Constant references to "Bactrians and Sacæ" in one breath, as it were, in Herodotus[4] point strongly to the coexistence of an aboriginal and Iranian population in Bactria. We hear of them as an obstinate and valiant race,[5] who were unaffected

---

[1] In nearly every case we find the conquering Aryan-speaking people forming a military aristocracy, who owe their supremacy over a more numerous aboriginal race to their superior weapons and organization. This is equally true of early Greece, Rome, and Gaul.

[2] Herod., VII. 64. *Vide supra*, p. 31.

[3] Quintus Curtius, VII. 6 : " Erant autem vii millia equitum, quorum auctoritatem ceteri sequebantur " ; " xxx millia," VII. 4.

[4] *E.g.*, VII. 54 and IX. 113.

[5] Quintus Curtius, IV. 6, 3. So, too, the author of the *Periplus* talks of the (later) Bactrians as a μαχιμώτατον ἔθνος.

by the luxury which enervated the Persian Empire
in its latter days. Rough and outspoken, they had
all the virtues of the ancient Persians. Like all
borderers, they were continually at war, and this kept
their martial spirit alive. Their life was one long
struggle to keep the Scythians from over the Oxus
from harrying their fields; they were independent
and apt to resent an insult, but intensely proud of
the privilege of having a royal prince as their ruler.
For him they would fight to the last, even against
the Great King; but on the whole they were the most
loyal and devoted of the subjects of the Persian
throne. At Gaugamela and after they resisted
Alexander to the last gasp, resenting bitterly the
intrusion of a foreigner who despised and suppressed
their most cherished customs. The satrapy of Bactria
was, strategically, the most important post in the
Empire; upon its holder devolved the duty, not
only of guarding against invasion from India on the
north, but of putting down revolts against the king
in Margiana, Aria, or other provinces, and upholding
his authority in these distant realms. Bactria, the
home of Zarathustra, was conservative in its religious
customs, and was very probably the scene of the
authorship of many of the oldest hymns of the
Zend Avesta. The Bactrians were famous for their
pithy proverbial sayings, of which two at least have
passed into current use. Cobares, the Iranian chief,

Curtius says : " Sunt autem Bactriani inter illas gentes promptissimi, horridis ingeniis, multumque a Persarum luxu abhorrentibus : siti haud procul Scytharum gente bellicosissima et
rapto vivere assueti, semperque in armis erant."

when speaking of Alexander to Bessus, remarked:
" His bark is worse than his bite : for still waters
run deep."[1]

AUTHORITIES.

Principally Strabo and Quintus Curtius. For the subject
of Anaitis and the Sacæa, see the interesting theories of
J. G. Frazer, *The Golden Bough*, ii. 24, 253, and iii. 151, etc.
(second edition). Dr. Frazer shows that the ceremonies of the
Sacæa bear an organic resemblance to those of Merodach at
Babylon and the Roman Saturnalia. The two latter were New
Year festivals, and at all three the " mocking " was the central
figure. The Jewish festival of Purim was of a similar nature
(Dr. Frazer sees an allusion to it in the story of Haman and
Mordecai). See also Ed. Meyer's article " Anaitis " in Roscher's
Lexicon, and Windischmann's *Study of Anaitis and Mithra*.

Practically nothing has been done towards the elucidation of
the many problems connected with the ethnology and geography
of Bactria. A mysterious city called Zariaspa is often mentioned. Strabo constantly identifies it with Bactra. Pliny
agrees, and states that Bactra is a *later* name for Zariaspa,
taken from the River Bactrus, on which the town stands.[2]
This is certainly wrong, Bactra being the Greek corruption of
Bâkhdhi, the earliest (and only) name for the city in Iranian
literature.

Professor Bury thinks Bactra and Zariaspa were double
capitals, like Sogdiana and Maracanda. He follows F. von
Schwarz in identifying Zariaspa with Chargui on the Oxus, a
good deal to the north-west. The termination *aspa* (Skt. *asva*)
is common in Persian names, both of places and persons—*e.g.*,

---

[1] "Adjicit deinde quod apud Bactrianos vulgo usurpabant :
*canem timidum vehementius latrare quam mordere ; altissima
quoque flumina minimo sono labi.*" (Quintus Curtius, VII. 4).
The proverbial sayings of the Bactrians were well known.
"Truthful words are always better" ("Honesty is the best
policy") is the dictum of a "wise man of Balkh" (Shâhnâma,
Trans. Mohl., vii. 44).

[2] Hist. Nat., VI. 18.

Hystaspes, Adraspa, etc.   Perhaps Zariaspa is the "City of the Golden Horse" [*zara*=gold ; *cf.* Zarafshan, "bringing down gold," the name of a river in Sogdiana, which, says Strabo, the Greeks paraphrased (παρωνόμασαν) by the word Πολυτίμητος].

See Adolf Holm, *Greek History*, i. 25, n. 1 (Eng. trans.); F. von Schwarz, *Alexander des grossen Feldzüge in Turkestan.*

CHAPTER II

In some remote period, probably about two thousand
years before Christ, the collection of tribes which
formed the nucleus of the Iranian and Indo-Aryan
races[1] swept, by a series of wave-like invasions,
into Western Asia. We have no data by which to
determine their route; they may have come across
the Jaxartes from the north-east; they may, possibly,
have even found their way across the Caucasus. It is
more probable, however, that they dwelt, before their
inruption into their final abode, somewhere between the
Aral and Caspian Seas, in the country occupied later
by the Dahæ. The invaders may be conveniently
divided into two groups—the Aryans and Iranians.
The Aryans were evidently the first to enter Iran,
whence they were driven southwards by the presence
of further invaders in their rear, who gradually forced
them across the Paropamisus into the Panjab, just as,

---

[1] I use the word "Iranian" to indicate the Persians, Medes,
Bactrians, and other tribes of *Iran*. By "Aryan" I signify
the kindred races of Northern India, the Vedic Hindus. But
the words "Iranian" and "Aryan" are philologically identical,
of course (Avesta, *Airiya*; Skt., *Ấrya*).

18

many centuries later, the Scythians forced southwards the Bactrian Greeks. The invading hordes
who followed, the nucleus of the Iranian race, appear
to have split into two bodies.[1] One body proceeded in
a westerly direction, and found a lodgment on the
eastern borders of the great Semitic nations of the
Tigris and Euphrates Valley. Of these, one powerful
tribe, the Persians, spread over the mountainous district at the head of the Persian Gulf; another, the
Median tribe, subdivided into several smaller clans,
occupied the dales and valleys of the country from the
shores of the Caspian to the land of Persis. Into the
rich valleys beyond they dared not penetrate; on the
other hand, the Assyrian troopers would hardly venture
to attack the hardy mountaineers in their fastnesses,
from which they only descended in search of plunder.
Later, the Medes overran Armenia. Some time before
the seventh century we find the original Turanian
population replaced by an Iranian one.

The other body of Iranian tribes proceeded in an
easterly direction. Forcing their predecessors and
kinsmen, the Aryans, to seek new homes over the
mountains, they proceeded to settle wherever the presence of ample streams provided a prospect of good

[1] This theory may be summarized as follows: The invading
Iranians split into two streams, which flowed east and west of
the Carmanian desert. The Eastern Iranians settled in Sogdiana, Bactria, Carmania, Margiana, and Aria. They drove
their predecessors, the Aryans, into India. The Western
Iranians went to the west of the desert. The foremost tribe
was the Persian; it was followed by the Medes, from whom
the Indo-Germanic settlers in Phrygia and Armenia may have
been offshoots.

pasture and tillage. The most powerful of these tribes took up their abode on the banks of the Oxus. They subdued the wandering nomads, and seized the ancient shrine of Bactra, which became their capital; some of their kinsmen even migrated into the vast and lonely country beyond the Oxus, and reached the banks of the Jaxartes. Being few in number, and, unlike their kinsmen of the west, dwelling in a level country with no mountains to protect them, the Bactrians seized the curious rocky eminences which rose abruptly here and there out of the flat alluvial plains. Here the Iranian lords built their castles, and dwelt in proud isolation. With their swift cavalry, they could swoop down upon an invader and retire as quickly to their strongholds, many of which were actually small towns, and quite impregnable.

Between the Aryan tribes which crossed the mountains and found a home in the Indus Valley and their Iranian kinsmen on the banks of the Oxus there was at first no great difference of language, customs, or religion. Both alike worshipped the powers of Nature, which to them were the visible signs of "something far more deeply interfused,"—Varuna, Οὐρανός, the shining vault of Heaven;[1] Mitra, the "friendly" light of the sun; Vâyu, the wind that drives away the storms, and makes bright the face of Heaven; Yama, the primeval man, reigning over the blessed souls in Paradise. Both alike celebrated the mysterious sacrament of the Sôma, when the sacred juice was solemnly consumed, to the spiritual uplifting of gods and men.

[1] "The Persians called the whole vault of the sky Zeus—*i.e.*, the Supreme God" (Herodotus, I. 131).

The two races, however, drifted farther and farther apart. The Aryans of the Panjab spread eastwards towards the banks of the Ganges, and lost touch with their northern kinsfolk. The rift is exemplified by the gradual changes which creep into the meaning of what were once common words to both tongues : *asura*, originally used to signify a " spirit," takes, among the Vedic Indians, the connotation of " demon," while the Iranians exalt it by applying it to the Supreme Intelligence, Ahura Mazda, the " Omniscient Lord." On the other hand, the word *deva*, originally used of the bright spirits of air and sky, and retaining that meaning in Sanskrit, is used in the Avesta tongue in the sense of " demons." It has been thought by some authorities that this strange opposition of meanings points to a time of strife between the Iranian and Vedic peoples, when the gods of the one became, like their *protégés*, the national foes of their opponents, and it is possible that this strife may have led to the great migration of the defeated tribes to the Panjab. Such a theory has nothing to support it but its inherent plausibility ; it is not in itself essential to explain the strange divergence in meaning of certain words of the common Aryan vocabulary, as such differences are often merely the work of lengthy separation.

Of the early history of Bactria we know little or nothing ; the lists of kings and accounts of their exploits given by the Sassanian and later writers are almost entirely a mass of untrustworthy legends. All we can glean for certain is that as early as the second millennium B.C., a powerful confederacy, of which

Bactria was the centre, existed in East Iran; the inhabitants, not crushed by the proximity of powerful neighbours, like their Persian and Median kinsmen, were yet prevented from sinking into a state of slothful ease by constant wars to repel the incursions of the Turanian nomads. They dwelt, a proud and powerful aristocracy, mostly in their acropolis-like strongholds, to which they retired when hard pressed, and from which their chivalry descended to chastise the marauders. We may imagine that they ruled in a similar style to the Norman barons in England, keeping in subjection a numerous helot population by virtue of their superior organization and intelligence; such, indeed, was the state of most countries in the early days of their invasion by the Aryan-speaking peoples. The capital of this great Iranian Empire was the ancient shrine of Bactra, probably chosen because the invaders already found it a place of great and immemorial sanctity.

The only episode in the early history of Bactria which appears to be founded upon fact is the story of the coming of the Iranian prophet, Zarathustra Spitama. Round his name, as round that of many of the great law-givers of the ancient world, such a plentiful crop of legends has sprung up, that many have doubted his existence altogether. There is, however, no reason to suppose that he was any less an actual personage than Lycurgus or Moses, although it is impossible at this distance to distinguish precisely what the Iranian religion actually owes to his teaching. His birthplace was somewhere in Media,[1] and he belonged to a tribe, the Magu, who had inherited or acquired, we know not how, a monopoly in religious functions. By this time the Iranian religion, like the Iranian language, had begun to diverge widely from its original Aryan prototype. As we have seen, the early Aryans worshipped the elements—the sacred fire (the Hindu Agni), the wide heavens, the sôma plant, the air, and the water. The Iranians developed certain aspects of this religious system, especially the worship of the sacred fire, and out of reverence for it abandoned the old practice of burning the dead, substituting the custom of exposing them instead to the birds.

This feeling of the necessity of keeping the sacred elements free from defilement further led to the elaboration of a great number of ritual observances of the most minute and, to modern eyes, often puerile character. Lists of clean and unclean animals and insects (the former, strangely enough, including the dog, almost universally looked upon as unclean), to be protected or destroyed, were formulated, and drastic penalties, consisting of fines and corporal punishment, were enacted to enforce the keeping of these rules. Lastly, the great central idea of the Iranian faith, the existence of a dualism in Nature, appeared; the Iranian explained Evil as the work of Ahriman, Angra Mainyu, the Prince of Darkness, and the Lord of the Hosts of Devas.[2]

[1] Probably at Raghæ, or Rai (Ραγαί), in Media Atropatene.
[2] This may have been acquired from contact with the Semitic nations.

That this creed was developed by the priestly caste of the Medes appears to be extremely probable; the minute code of the Vendidâd was certainly not meant for the populace at large, where at best it would be "more honoured in the breach than the observance"; and, as we know, its most important precept was violated by the Persian kings themselves, who were buried in the royal sepulchre at Pasargadæ, and not exposed at all.[1] Other indications, such as the silence of classical writers on the subject of Ahriman, seem to point to the existence of a distinct Magian creed, only partially accepted by the Iranians generally.

Such was the "reformed religion" which Zarathustra, apparently, propagated. Tradition says it was in the reign of one Gustaspa[2] that he appeared at "Bactra the beautiful, city of the high-streaming banners," the ancient seat of the monarchs of Eastern Iran. Apparently he was not alone, for his wife's relations are said to have attained high positions in the royal court. This may have led to the widespread adoption of his tenets; and so powerful did the family of Spitama become at Bactra, that henceforth that city became the centre of Zoroastrianism, the heart of the new creed, and a legend grew up in Greece that "Zoroaster was a Bactrian

[1] The body was, however, coated with wax to prevent actual contact with the soil (Herodotus, I. 140).

[2] Conjectures as to the date of Zoroaster vary to an astounding degree. Some identify Gustaspa with the father of Darius; others put him back to 1400 B.C. or earlier, or declare him to be a myth. Professor Jackson, of Columbia University, thinks he flourished during the Medic supremacy, and to have died about 583 B.C.

king."[1] Finally, according to Firdousi, he perished
in one of the many Scythian invasions. The
barbarians are said to have penetrated into Balkh
itself, and to have killed the prophet before his
fire-altar.

We must now turn our attention to the Western
Iranians. About 700 B.C. the Medes at last found an
opportunity to break away from the Assyrian yoke.
Phraortes, some fifty years later, united the Persian
and Median kingdoms, and the doom of Nineveh was
sealed. From the wreck of the Empire of Assyria
arose two new nations, Babylon and Media. At first
the two races, absorbed in their respective conquests,
remained at peace with one another ; Nebuchadnezzar
was busy with his Jewish and Egyptian expeditions,
while the Medes were pushing forward to the Halys.
For a time Lydia staved off the inevitable doom, and
a treaty was made between the rival nations, and
ratified by a marriage between the Medic king and a
Lydian princess. Hopes of peace from this alliance,
however, were cast to the winds when, in 550 B.C.,
an event of the utmost import in the history of
Iran took place. The ancient Medic line was deposed
by the Persians, and Cyrus the Great, the first of the

---

[1] I have said nothing of the legendary wars of Ninus and
Semiramis against Bactria. The Assyrians never invaded
Bactria, much less conquered a Bactrian king called variously
Zoroaster (Justin) and Oxyartes (Diodorus). The story found
in Justin and many writers originated in a Persian legend
retailed by Ctesias. Eugène Wilhelm, in a learned pamphlet
(Louvain, 1891), shows that Zoroaster and Oxyartes are cor-
ruptions of some name like Ζαθραύστης, itself a Grecism of an
Iranian word.

Achæmenids, became king of the now extensive
Perso-Median Empire. The fall of Sardis, under the
attacks of the new monarch, speedily followed, and
with Sardis, the overthrow of the Greek colonies on
the Asiatic coastline. Finally, in 538, the once
despised Iranians stormed the mighty city of Babylon,
and proclaimed themselves the masters of Western
Asia.

It was not likely that under these circumstances
the East Iranians would long maintain their position
of proud isolation from the doings of their western
kinsmen. Soon after the fall of Babylon Cyrus
undertook a great expedition to the East. Bactria,
together with the minor East Iranian tribes, willingly
submitted to the conqueror of Media, and the Iranians
were now for the first time incorporated into a single
vast empire. Cyrus was not slow in perceiving that
one of the chief menaces to his great kingdom lay in
the Scythians on the north-east border. In order to
settle the country as far as possible, he plunged into
Sogdiana, and attempted to drive the nomads back
across the Jaxartes.[1] He was temporarily successful
in this attempt, and before retiring established a
great frontier fortress, called Cyropolis by the Greeks,
to keep guard over the border. Seeing the impossibility of governing Bactria from the distant
capital of Susa, Cyrus started the practice, afterwards adopted by his successors, of placing Bactria
under a prince of the blood, who acted as the king's
viceroy. The first of these royal satraps was his son

---

[1] Ctesias, of course, embroiders the story of the campaign
with various romantic (and utterly fabulous) stories.

Smerdis.[1] This measure effectually conciliated the pride of the haughty and turbulent Bactrians, as it gave their country a sort of pre-eminence over its neighbours; the satraps of Bactria appear to have always enjoyed the devoted adherence of their subjects. Thus Bactria became, like the Deccan under the Moghuls, an excellent school for young princes. The office was no sinecure, owing to the continual threats of invasion from over the border.

It is related by Arrian,[2] that from Bactria Cyrus went southwards across the Paropamisus and reduced Kapisa (North-East Afghanistan). From here he marched into the Panjab and tried, with terrible results, to perform the feat, afterwards accomplished by Alexander with equally disastrous consequences, of marching home by the southern route across the tropical deserts of Gedrosia (the modern Mekran). Strabo disbelieves this story, and it seems probable that Arrian is confusing his exploits with those of Darius. Cyrus was killed in a second expedition across the Jaxartes against the Massa Getæ, who appear to have given trouble on the Bactrian border.

He was succeeded by Cambyses, who appears to have devoted all his time to Egypt, and to have left the eastern portion of the Empire to itself. The reign of Cambyses was chiefly remarkable for the extraordinary growth of the influence of the Magi, who, like the Brahmans of India, aspired to become the "power behind the throne" in Persia. Smerdis, satrap of Bactria, the king's younger

---

[1] Ctesias calls him Tanoxyarces.
[2] *Exped. Alex.*, vi. 24.

brother, had been secretly made away with, probably
because, like other governors of that distant province, he had shown signs of desiring to set himself
up as an independent ruler. This treacherous
act brought its own reward. No one knew for
certain that Smerdis was dead, and thus the Magi,
profiting by the prolonged absence of Cambyses,
were able to set up one of their own number as
king, pretending that he was the dead prince.
The conspiracy assumed such gigantic proportions
that Cambyses, in a fit of despair, killed himself;
and for over a year the false Smerdis (or rather,
the crafty priests who used him as their puppet),
reigned supreme. Finally a conspiracy, headed
by Darius, son of Prince Hystaspes (Vistaspa)
governor of Hyrcania and Parthia, was formed,
which overthrew the usurper and his party. To
crush a rebellion in a huge, nebulous, and little-
organized empire of the extent of Persia, was no easy
matter; pretenders sprang up from Babylon to
Armenia, and it was only after two years' fighting
that peace was restored, and the Magi made to pay
with their blood for their bold attempt. It was
probably to prevent a recurrence of similar disturb-
ances that Darius set about the gigantic scheme of
reform by which he linked his vast possessions into a
co-ordinated whole, paying fixed assessments to the
Royal Treasury, and connected with the capital by
that wonderful network of roads, with their service of
posts, so efficiently maintained that the news of a
rising could be instantly conveyed and troops rapidly
moved to the disturbed area. Darius finally divided the

empire into satrapies, each paying a fixed sum to the Imperial Treasury; this wise precaution prevented local governors from levying taxes at will, under the pretext that they were required by the Imperial Government.

Under the new scheme, Bactria became the twelfth satrapy in the empire, and paid an annual tribute of 360 talents (about £90,000). This seems a small contribution, compared to the sum of 1,000 talents contributed by the most wealthy province, Assyria; but it may be that Bactria received concessions of some kind in return for its loyalty to Darius.

Darius, as we have already mentioned, was the son of the governor of a great province of Eastern Iran, and he appears to have won the esteem of the Bactrians, which may account for the remarkable fact that these ardent champions of the Zoroastrian creed did not join the side of the Magi in any of the various risings. This may be also partly due to the fact that the satrapy of Bactria was in the hands of a certain Dardases, who appears to have remained loyal to his master's cause in spite of grave temptations. One of the most formidable of the rebellions confronting Darius was that of Phraortes of Margiana, who proclaimed himself to be a descendant of the ancient Median kings. Even Hystaspes was unable to quell the rising, which was finally subdued by the king in person, in co-operation with the Bactrians. The Behistun inscription records how Darius sent word to "Dardases his servant" to "smite the people that owned him not." Dardases was probably a prince of the blood, like the other Bactrian satraps, but except from this solitary reference, we hear nothing further of him.

About 512 B.C. an important expedition left Bactria
for the Indus Valley.[1] Scylax of Caryanda in Caria
undertook the exploration of the course of the Indus
from the land of the Pakhtu[2] to the sea, and returned,
after a most adventurous voyage of over a year, via the
Red Sea, landing near the modern port of Suez. A
province south of the Paropamisus was established,
probably as a subsatrapy of Bactria, and a regular
trade was opened from the mouth of the Indus up the
Persian Gulf. One of the many important results of
this undertaking was to open up a connection between
the Persians and their long-forgotten kinsmen of the
Panjab. Probably, historians have never appreciated
the significance of this contact. One tangible result,
at any rate, was the introduction into the north-west
of India of the Kharoshthi script, which is evidently
of Aramaic origin. It continued in use for over 800
years on the border, till ousted, about A.D. 343, by
the Brahmi (or Brahmin) writing, the parent of the
modern Indian alphabets.

In the reign of Xerxes, who succeeded to the throne
in 485 B.C., two of his brothers, Masistes and Hystaspes,
appear to have dwelt at Bactra. Masistes, apparently
the elder, was satrap of the province, while upon
Hystaspes devolved the command of the troops, and in
this capacity he took charge of the Bactro-Sacean con-

---

[1] Herodotus, IV. 44. The so-called *Periplus* of Scylax is a
later work.

[2] The Afghans (Pushtu). The expedition started from
" Kaspatyrus and the country of Paktyiké," probably at the
junction of the Kabul River with the Indus. Kaspatyrus is the
" Kaspapyrus " of Hekataeus, " a city of Gandhara." Perhaps
the Indian name was Kaspapur.

tingent during the Grecian expedition of 480 B.C. Apparently, the Bactrian brigade comprised two distinct bodies of troops ; the infantry consisted largely of semi-savage aboriginals, "armed with short spears and bows of Bactrian cane,"—singularly ineffective weapons, one would think, with which to attack the Greek hoplite ; while the cavalry was composed of the Iranian equites. The latter, being not very different from the Persian horse, are not mentioned in the picturesque catalogue of the seventh book of the history of Herodotus. It is noteworthy, however, that when Mardonius was selecting a picked force to carry on the campaign after the death of Xerxes, he chose "Medes, Sacæ, Bactrians and Indians, both infantry and cavalry,"[1] which testifies to the military prowess of the Bactrian army. We shall not be far wrong if we imagine that the Bactrian cavalry were principally retained ; the footmen with their cane bows would only be useful as skirmishers, and were hardly likely to make much impression against the hoplite, with his long pike, heavy armour, and close formations. Masistes also took part in the campaign on the staff of Mardonius, and on his return to Sardis after the Battle of Mycalé lost his life in a characteristic fashion. The queen, suspecting an intrigue between Xerxes and his brother's wife, contrived to seize her wretched rival and put her to death in a barbarous manner. Masistes fled to Bactria vowing to raise the satrapy and take condign vengeance, but was intercepted by cavalry and put to death, with his family and escort.[2] Hystaspes succeeded to the vacant post. Apparently, he did not

---

[1] Herodotus, VIII. 113.　　　　[2] *Ibid.*, VII. 108.

venture to take any measures at once to avenge the insult; but upon the death of Xerxes, in 464, he promptly
revolted against Artaxerxes Longimanus, and was only
subdued after two pitched battles.[1]

From the death of Xerxes to the invasion of Alexander the history of Bactria is almost a blank for us.
Herodotus ends his story at the battle of Mycalé, and
Xenophon, our next authority on the subject of Persia,
has little or nothing to tell us about the condition of
Eastern Iran. Bactria appears to have remained a
flourishing and prosperous state, unaffected by the
degeneracy which was fast overtaking the western
kingdom. Either Artaxerxes I. or his successor of the
same name appears to have been a devotee of the
Bactrian Anahid, and to have adorned her temple with
the magnificent star-crowned statue, which is mentioned so often in later literature.

Bactria seems to have been used as a sort of
" Siberia " under the Persian kings. Before the battle
of Ladé the Persian commanders tried to frighten the
rebels into submission with threats of " banishment to
Bactria" in case they failed to yield. Ordinarily, it has
been remarked, the Greek maidens, at any rate, would
have been sent to Susa: but Bactria is mentioned because it would appear more distant and terrible to the
Greeks, who all exaggerated the size of the Persian
empire.[2]

A colony of Libyans from Barca was settled by
Darius in Bactria;[3] we never hear of them again. We

---

[1] Compare Diodorus, XI. 69, with what Ctesias tells us.
[2] Herodotus, VI. 9 ; and see Rawlinson's note.
[3] *Ibid.*, IV. 204.

shall, however, meet with the descendants of the Branchidæ (settled by Xerxes on the north bank of the Oxus) under tragic circumstances. They had been guilty of betraying the Temple of Apollo at Didymi to the Persians, and were removed hither to escape the vengeance of their Greek neighbours.

AUTHORITIES.

Of the ancient authorities, Herodotus holds the first place. Justin repeats legends from Ctesias, usually worthless. Equally unreliable are the Persian authorities—Firdousi, and others. For Iranian customs, see the translations of the Vendidâd, *Sacred Books of the East*, iv. and xxxi., with valuable prefaces by Darmsteter and Mills.

Of modern authorities, Rawlinson (*Five Great Oriental Monarchies*) is still valuable. Von Gutschmid's articles in the ninth edition of the *Encyclopædia Britannica*, and his *Geschichte Irans*, are noteworthy, and also the up-to-date articles on "Zoroaster" and "Ancient Persia" in the latest edition of the *Encyclopædia*, by Karl Geldner and Ed. Meyer.

CHAPTER III

In 334 b.c. came the day of reckoning for Persia. The magnificent organization of the empire by Darius the Great had merely earned for him the title of the " shopkeeper " from the Persian nobility, and corruption and intrigue had reduced the greatest kingdom of antiquity to a huge unwieldy mass of States, still possessing enormous resources, but incapable of utilizing them. The hardy Persian mountaineers of two centuries before had become as luxurious and enervated as the alien nations they had displaced. The corruption, however, had not spread across the Carmanian Desert, and the Bactrians of the East, owing to their constant wars with the Scythians, and their great distance from Susa, retained in their far-off rugged country some of the virtues of the primitive Iranians of the days of Cyrus the Great.

The Viceroy of Bactria at the time of Alexander's invasion was Bessus, a distant cousin of Darius Codomannus. It was hardly likely that he would have much respect for the mild, weak prince, a puppet in the hands of the conspirators who had raised him to a dignity for which he had small ability or inclination. By this time, indeed, Bactria had drifted into the position of a semi-independent kingdom, little disposed to tolerate interference from the capital. As a matter of fact, the Persian kings, fully occupied as they were with their ceaseless round of intrigues and wars with Greece, had of late years had no time to meddle in their eastern provinces; nor would the Bactrians have brooked any attempt to bring them into line. Devoted to their satraps, they were always ready to follow them, if an ambitious prince showed any disposition to strike for independence.

It is significant to notice that only 1,000 Bactrian cavalry took part in the great battle of Gaugamela,[1] a decisive struggle, to which one would have thought all the forces of the empire would have rallied. They fought, it is true, with the utmost gallantry. They opened the battle with a brilliant charge upon the Greek right, which was well pushed home, and for a time effectually checked the advance of the enemy. Alexander was compelled to run the risk of seriously weakening his centre before he was able to beat off this dangerous flank attack. But the fact remains that only a small Bactrian contingent took part in the engagement. No doubt Bessus was already awaiting a favourable opportunity for raising the standard of revolt, and had excellent reasons for lending his kinsman only a very perfunctory support.

In the spring of 330 B.C., when the ancient capital of the Persians had fallen into the hands of the Macedonians, the final pursuit of Darius began. It

[1] October 1, 331 B.C.

was felt that the last chance lay in falling back upon Eastern Iran. The great provinces of Bactria, Ariana, and Margiana, were as yet unaffected by the invasion; but the unfortunate Darius was now little more than a prisoner in the hands of Bessus. From Ecbatana to Ragæ, from Ragæ to the Caspian gates, fled the unhappy monarch and his guardians, his forces melting away as he went. Alexander spared neither men nor horses in his wild pursuit. At last, one summer morning, after a desperate night ride of nearly fifty miles, with a few picked troopers he rode into the enemy's rearguard as dawn was breaking. The foe scattered at the onset; a few miles further on Alexander found the last of the heirs of "Cyrus the King, the Achæmenian," lying among his dead mules and drivers, stabbed through and through. Bessus was far ahead, flying to Bactria to proclaim himself king under the title of Artaxerxes.

Alexander now entered upon the most difficult part of the Persian campaign. He was no longer at war with an effete and disorganized empire; he was face to face with the primitive Iranians of East Persia, hardy warriors still retaining some of the virtues of the mountaineers who had conquered Assyria and Babylon, and whose simplicity and courage had won the admiration of the Greeks themselves. He had to march thousands of miles through an unknown country, across burning deserts and lofty mountains, where at any moment he might perish for want of food or water, or be cut off by a rising in his rear. But the splendid Macedonian force never hesitated. Hyrcania, the wooded country on the Caspian shore, was first subdued, and word was given to Parmenio to send a force to occupy this important point on the line of communications. A move was then made to Zadracarta, where a halt was called, and a concentration of the forces for an advance on Bactra was effected. Alexander's transport arrangements must have been admirable, for within a fortnight, notwithstanding the fact that the king and his little body of cavalry had travelled hundreds of miles ahead of the main army in pursuit of Darius, all was ready to push forward.

Alexander had determined to advance by the great caravan route which runs through Susa and Merv to Bactra, along which water and provisions would be easily obtainable. Hardly, however, had he disappeared into the desert beyond Susa when Satibarzanes, satrap of Aria, who had lulled his suspicions by a pretended submission, revolted, hoping, no doubt, to cut off his line of communication. Satibarzanes was a confederate of Bessus, and the design was to take the advancing Macedonians in flank and rear at once. It was a highly critical moment, for Satibarzanes was certain of the help of Barsaentes of Drangiana. Once more Alexander's marvellous speed in moving troops saved the situation; he turned abruptly south, and dashed down to Artocoana (Herat) in two days. His unexpected appearance struck terror into the enemy. Satibarzanes galloped away in hot haste to Bactra; Barsaentes was surrendered and executed.

Alexander now altered his plans. He determined to attack Bactra from the south, subduing the pro-

vinces *en route*, and founding colonies on the line
of march to secure his rear. It was a terribly daring
policy, but Alexander knew his own powers. The
winter 330-329 B.C. was passed in Gedrosia. The
idea was to cross the mountains as soon the passes
were open, so as to enter the formidable deserts of
southern Bactria before the hot weather made them
impassable. In the early spring of 329 the columns
began to march up the Helmand Valley. The remainder of the year was spent in advancing to the
foot of the Paropamisus. Two prolonged halts were
made : once in Arachosia, where a city was founded,
which may still survive in the modern Kandahar, and
once again at the foot of the actual defiles, where
another veteran colony, numbering 7,000, was established. By this means the retreat was secured, and
all chances of a revolt in the Macedonian rear were
prevented. In the meantime Alexander was rejoined
by a force from Aria, bringing the welcome news
that they had defeated and killed Satibarzanes.

Now began one of the most stupendous of Alexander's tasks. In front of him lay the vast unexplored
ranges of the Hindu-Kush, with their precipitous
gorges and pathless glaciers. It was a task more
formidable than Hannibal's ; but the soldiers, though
often reduced to raw mutton and the fœtid silphium-
root for sustenance, finally emerged triumphant upon
the Bactrian plains. A prolonged halt was made
at the frontier fortress of Drapsaca, the scattered
forces were reorganized, and a move was made in the
direction of Aornus. The sudden appearance of the
Macedonians over the mountains appears to have

utterly demoralized the foe, already perturbed by the
fate of their Arian allies under Satibarzanes. The
Bactrian cavalry had mobilized to the number of
8,000, and now was their chance, when the enemy,
disorganized by their privations and with most of
their horses lying dead in the high passes, were
debouching in detached columns upon the lower
levels. But the Macedonians had acquired that
prestige which is so invaluable to a commander.
Nothing would face them; henceforward Alexander's
foes, until he came to India, where the terror of his
name had not yet spread, would only stand up to
him behind strong walls, and not in open battle. It
is strange that Alexander should have been permitted
to enter the gates of Bactra, the sacred stronghold of
Zoroastrianism, without a blow. This famous city on
other occasions offered to invaders the most desperate
resistance recorded in the history of the ancient
world, as its natural and artificial defences well
enabled it to do. It must have been with feelings
of more than ordinary interest that the war-worn
generals looked round this remote yet famous town,
which to Greeks of the last generation was so distant
that it was spoken of as a semi-legendary place, on the
confines of the world. But Bactra appears to have
disappointed the Greeks, who, with their usual con-
tempt for the "barbarian," noted with disapproval
the revolting customs prevalent among the lower
orders. The Saceans gave over their dead to dogs,
and even allowed the infirm and old to suffer the
same fate—their bones littered the streets. Nor did
the Zoroastrian custom of exposing corpses to the

birds meet their approval, and Alexander promptly ordered the *dakhmas*, or Towers of Silence, to be closed.

Again the army made a brief halt. The situation was distressing enough. In the rear rumours of rebellion were rife, and it was doubtful if Erygius, an old and not very active general, was capable of the vast task of keeping open the lines of communication. Owing to the state of the country, it was difficult to procure remounts to replace the horses lost in the mountains, and cavalry, in view of the enemy's mobility, was an absolute essential. But the first thing to be done was to crush Bessus before he should succeed in raising a formidable force in Sogdiana, whither he had fled. Once again Alexander advanced in pursuit. The journey from Bactra to the Oxus was short, but terribly trying. The hot weather had set in, and in spite of the precaution of marching at night, the troops arrived at the river bank half dead with thirst and exhaustion, for Bessus had taken the precaution to break down the bridges and destroy the provisions and wells during his retreat. Alexander very characteristically refused to drink or even unbuckle his armour till the last straggler had come in. We can well imagine his pride in the splendid troops who could overcome alike the intense cold of the passes of the Hindu-Kush and the horrors of a forced march through the Mid-Asian deserts in the height of summer. Bessus had burnt the boats; but the Oxus was crossed on skins stuffed with straw, and the army set foot in Sogdiana.

It was at this juncture that one of the most disgraceful incidents in Alexander's career took place, so utterly inexcusable that his biographers were ashamed to record it.[1] On the northern bank of the Oxus dwelt the little colony of Greeks descended from those Branchidæ who had been deported thither by Xerxes to save them from the fury of the Milesians after the Persian wars. They streamed out in a joyous crowd to welcome, in broken Greek, the coming of their kinsmen; but Alexander savagely ordered them to be surrounded and massacred. His reason was that their ancestors[2] had betrayed the Hellenic cause, and he, as the champion of Hellenic rights, was bound to avenge the wrong. It was precisely by such acts that Alexander showed how little he was imbued with the true Greek spirit; under the thin veneer of Hellenism lay the barbarian, ready to break out, on the smallest provocation, in ugly forms of senseless brutality.

Alexander's advance over the Oxus had caused a further panic in the Bactrian camp. No obstacle, it seemed, would stop him; and the Sogdian confederates of Bessus, Spitamenes and Dataphernes, decided to betray their leader, hoping thereby to pacify the invader and put an end to further conquests in this region. Bessus was handed over to Ptolemy Lagus, and doomed to horrible, but not undeserved tortures; but Alexander was not to be diverted from his purpose so easily. He saw that

---

[1] The story is only found in Curtius. There is, unfortunately, no reason to doubt it.

[2] Five generations had elapsed since the original misdeed.

nothing less than the complete subjection of Iran would make an advance on India possible.

The Macedonians advanced rapidly. Maracanda, the royal capital, fell, with other strong fortresses, and received a garrison, and the army pushed on to the Jaxartes. Here Alexander determined to found the last of his great colonies, Alexandria Ultima, on the banks of this distant river, to keep watch over the Scythians, and to protect the great trade route to China.

Resistance, however, though scotched, was not yet killed. With the disappearance of the King in the wilds of the north a great national reaction set in. The movement was primarily a religious one. Alexander had shown himself the enemy of Zoroastrianism : the burial customs of the Iranians had been forbidden, libraries and temples ransacked, and the sacred Avesta books either destroyed, or, what was almost a worse desecration, translated into Greek by recreant Persians to satisfy the curiosity of Greek savants.

"Alexander the accursed " had aroused the deepest feelings of his enemies.[1] In Bactra the rumour was industriously circulated that a massacre of the Iranian knightly class was being planned,[2] which had the effect of stirring up considerable feeling against

[1] "Gazashté Alexander." The persecution of the Iranian religion is not mentioned by Greek writers. There is a persistent Persian tradition to this effect—e.g., J.B.B.R.A.S., xv., p. 37.

[2] Quintus Curtius, VII. 6 ; vide Arrian, iv. 1 sub fin. It is interesting to see the same story appearing in Persian sources in the apocryphal correspondence of Alexander and Aristotle, translated by Darmesteter, Journal Asiatique, 1894, vol. iii., pp. 185 ff. and 502 ff. (New Series).

Alexander's viceroy, Artabazus.   At the same time a fierce rising blazed up in Sogdiana.   Cyropolis and other cities put their Macedonian garrisons to the sword.   At Maracanda, Alexander's principal fortress, the citadel was fiercely beset, and the detachment scarcely able to hold its own.   The revolt was ably organized by Spitamenes, and so encouraging did the prospects of success appear, that Oxyartes and the other princes of Eastern Sogdiana, who had hitherto remained quiet, decided to throw in their lot with their countrymen.   The Sacæ, terrified at the rise of the great fortress commanding the ford over the Jaxartes, were mustering ominously on the further bank, and a body of troops from the Massa Getæ had gone to join Spitamenes.

A demonstration in force dispersed the nomads, and the builders of Further Alexandria were left in peace.   A force sent to relieve Maracanda was less lucky : they raised the siege, but in attempting to follow up their opponents were cleverly ambushed by Spitamenes and killed almost to a man.

In the meanwhile Alexander was busy with Cyropolis, which he eventually captured,[1] and on his advance Spitamenes and his horsemen vanished into the wilds. The fighting which was necessary to subdue the country resembles that which the British had to undertake for the conquest of the Deccan.   The Saceans and Bactrians, unable to face the Macedonians in the field, bade them defiance from their

---

[1] The inhabitants were sent to populate Alexandria Eschaté. For the various cities founded and destroyed by Alexander see Appendix V., p. 165 (*f*), and the passages of Strabo there quoted.

lofty rock-fortresses, which had to be stormed, often
with considerable loss. "Can you fly?" asked
Arimazes, the commandant of one of these strongholds, in answer to a summons to surrender.
Alexander convinced him that flying was not necessary by scaling, with a picked force of 300 men,
a rocky crag which commanded the city. The
garrison now surrendered, and Arimazes was crucified
as a warning to the rest. By this policy, partly of
coercion, partly of conciliation, Western Sogdiana
was subdued so effectually that Peucolaus was able
to keep order with a standing army of 3,000 men
only. A chain of forts from the Oxus to the Ochus,
where they joined hands with Alexandria Margiana,
"velut freni domitarum gentium," as Curtius says,
kept the western border subdued, and prevented any
incursions of the Dahæ, who were allies of Spitamenes. Alexandria Eschaté, now a formidable fortress,
effectually checked any similar diversions from the
north-east.

The result of these measures was seen when
Spitamenes was overtaken by the fate which, partly
through his instrumentality, had befallen Bessus.
He was betrayed by his confederates and murdered;
his head was sent to Alexander as a peace offering.[1]

The situation had thus improved considerably when
Alexander ordered his troops, at the end of 328, into
winter-quarters. It was not possible, however, to
leave the country as yet, as Eastern Sogdiana still held
out, and no operations were possible until the levies
from Macedonia arrived. Alexander's striking force

---

[1] Arrian, IV. 17 *fin.* Curtius says his wife murdered him.

must have become by this time very small indeed;
besides his recent losses in the field, an immense
number had been swallowed up by the numerous
garrison colonies established at points of vantage.
It was therefore decided for the winter months to
hold the royal court at Maracanda, a huge fortress
and palace, regarded as the ancient capital of the
country, and admirably adapted for the purpose.
Here[1] the unfortunate incident took place which cost
Clitus his life. Alexander, like all Macedonians, was
given to drinking, and the dryness of the climate is
alleged by some as an excuse for his excessive indul-
gence. It is hard, however, to blame the king particularly for his share in this disgraceful scene. At the
time of his murder Clitus was under orders to proceed
to Bactra[2] to take over charge from Artabazus, who
found that the post was beyond the capacity of a
man of his years. Artabazus does not appear to
have been a great success; Alexander's experiments
of putting natives in charge of important posts did
not always succeed. Clitus was now replaced by
Amyntas.

Early in 327, Alexander, having received his rein-
forcements, moved out for a final campaign in
Parætacene. The heart of the native opposition
centred round the gigantic fortress of Sisimithres, the
Sogdian rock, which commands the passes leading
into the country from the south. Here had assembled

[1] So Curtius. Arrian says the early part of the winter was
spent at Zariaspa. For a discussion of the identity of this
mysterious city, see Chapter I. *fin.*
[2] Curtius, VIII. 1 ; Arrian, IV. 17.

Oxyartes, a brother[1] of Darius, with his family—the last hope of the royal race—and round him clustered the remnants of Bactrian independence. But the Macedonians were now experts in mountain warfare, and surprised the citadel after a night attack. Among the captives was the beautiful Roxané,[2] daughter of Oxyartes. She was brought, with thirty other maidens, before the Macedonian chiefs as they sat at table. Her beauty so struck Alexander that, to the surprise of everyone, he there and then married her, after the simple Macedonian rite,[3] offering her bread divided with the sword, of which each partook. Alexander was usually indifferent to women, and it is impossible not to think that motives of policy had something to do with this romantic action. Marriage with a daughter of the royal race would go far to conciliate native opinion to his rule, for it had been Alexander's fixed claim since he first set foot in Persia that he was not a mere military invader, but the successor of the Achemænidæ upon the royal throne. Bactria was to be the base of his operations against India, and these would be impossible to carry out unless the country was completely settled. He also wished to set his veterans the example of marrying Persian wives, and making the new country their

[1] So Plutarch. Diodorus calls him "King of Bactria," and Firdousi says Roshanak is "Dara's daughter."

[2] *I.e.*, Roshan-ak, "little star." *Roshan*=light, star ; *-ak* is an "affectionate" diminutive.

[3] For the details, see Plutarch, *Alexander* (Langhorne's translation, p. 478); *Sikander Nama,* canto xxxiii.; Quintus Curtius, VIII. 4, 23 ; Arrian, *Anab.,* IV. 21. Also the passage of Strabo given in the Appendix, p. 165 (*f*).

homes, so as to secure his conquests permanently. He was followed by Seleucus, who married Apama, the daughter of the dead Spitamenes, and thus peculiarly qualified himself and his successors for the position they afterwards claimed. It cannot, however, be said that the alliance was popular with the Macedonian generals at large. Alexander on his return to Bactra was more autocratic than ever. Incited, perhaps, by his wife, he insisted on prostrations and other servile signs of obedience, after the Persian fashion, from the court. The resulting discontent led to the " Conspiracy of the Pages," as it was called. The conspiracy was, as usual, stamped out in blood. It cannot be said that Roxané got much happiness from her romantic marriage. Almost immediately after Alexander set out for India, whence he returned only to die. A few months after his death she bore him a son, Alexander Ægus, as he is meaninglessly called.[1] After Antipater's death mother and child fled to Epirus, only to be caught and cruelly murdered by Cassander.

Alexander might well have rested on his laurels after the stupendous achievements of the past three years. He had performed a feat which in any age would have been entitled to the admiration of mankind; at that time it was almost superhuman. He had literally conquered a new world, and not only conquered, but settled it. In spite of lines of communication 2,000 miles in length, he had never suffered a serious reverse. He had penetrated, without

---

[1] ΑΙΓΟΣ is a silly mistake for ΑΛΛΟΣ (*i.e.*, Alexander the Second).

maps or guides, over precipitous mountains and track-
less deserts, in the face of an active and warlike
enemy, and through the midst of hostile country.
None but a genius for organization, with a perfect
transport and a magnificently trained intelligence
department, could have done this. It has been
maintained that he never met with real resistance;
the truth was that in most cases his movements
were so rapid that he took his foe by surprise. The
Iranian was as stout a soldier as any in the ancient
world.

But there was no rest for Alexander. Spring saw
him busy with the preparations for a descent upon
India. The first thing to do was obviously to secure
his base. For this purpose an army of 11,500 was
posted at Bactra under Amyntas, while twelve
garrison towns were founded in Bactria and Sogdiana,
in which were placed the troops who were likely to
be refractory at the prospect of a further advance.[1]
They were a turbulent crowd, and must have num-
bered nearly 30,000 men. Some of them revolted
immediately after Alexander's departure, and tried
to set up a certain Athenodorus as their king. He
was murdered; whereupon a body of malcontents,
under a leader named Bico, left Bactria. Amyntas
probably made no effort to detain them.[2]

A much larger body, computed by some at 23,000,
also fled on receiving the news of Alexander's death.
They entered Media, where they were cut to pieces by

[1] Justin. XI. 6 *fin.*
[2] Curtius. IX. 7. He *may* be relating what really happened
after Alexander's death.

satrap Peithon, who probably had no alternative in dealing thus with his unwelcome visitors.[1]

In the meanwhile Bactria appears to have been fairly peaceful. Tyriaspes,[2] governor of Paropamisus and Kabul, was accused of extortion, and petitions were sent to Alexander for redress. They reached him on the Indus, and he sent back orders for the offender's execution. Tyriaspes was replaced by Oxyartes. Oxyartes had been suspected of complicity in the conspiracy of the pages, but, probably owing to the intercession of Roxané, had escaped.[3]

There is some ground for thinking that Amyntas, perhaps owing to the incompetence shown by him in dealing with the turbulent settlers, was superseded by Stasanor of Soli. Sogdiana, apparently, was then put in charge of "Philip the Prætor," governor of Parthia, who subsequently became satrap of Bactria as well. Oxyartes remained in charge of Kabul for some years, perhaps until the province was handed over by Seleucus Nicator to Chandragupta. Apparently, both he and Stasanor assumed a semi-independent position after Alexander's death.

AUTHORITIES.

Arrian and Curtius, and, incidentally, Justin and Strabo. Arrian is the most valuable. Their merits have been discussed in the Introduction.

---

[1] Diod. Sic., XVIII. 7.

[2] Tirystes, Arrian, VI. 15 ; Terioltes, Curtius, IX. 8.

[3] "Oxathres, prætor Bactrianorum, non absolutus modo sed etiam jure amplioris imperii donatus est " (Curtius).

CHAPTER IV

THE ESTABLISHMENT OF BACTRIAN INDEPENDENCE

On the death of Alexander, the huge edifice which the master-mind had built up melted away almost as quickly as it had sprung up into being. Alexander had done all that forethought and policy could suggest to consolidate his conquest on his march to the East, but he was removed before the schemes he had set in motion had time to mature. His officers had learned only too well the lessons which Alexander the general had to teach; Alexander the apostle of Hellenism, the founder of a cosmopolitan world-empire, they utterly failed to comprehend.[1]

At first Perdiccas, by virtue of his personal ascendancy, established a temporary *modus vivendi*, with himself as regent; he lacked, however, the magic personality of his great predecessor, and in a short time the mutual rivalry of the generals plunged Asia into war, Perdiccas himself finding his death on the banks of the Nile at the hands of his own troopers.

One of the most distressing of the effects of Alex-

---

[1] "It was the fond dream of each 'successor' of Alexander that in his person might, perhaps, be one day united *all* the territories of the great conqueror" (Rawlinson, *Sixth Oriental Monarchy*, chap. iii.).

ander's untimely end was that the Macedonian invasion of the East, instead of consolidating the various Asiatic nations into a great Hellenic State, in which the immense resources of the Persian Empire were turned to proper account, resulted merely in bitter discord and further disintegration. The Macedonian troops, who had marched across half a continent to accomplish what had been, perhaps, the greatest project which human enterprise has ever conceived, were now, as a reward for their labours, set at one another's throats, and the mild, if ineffective, government of the Achæmenids was exchanged for something infinitely worse—the tyranny of a foreign military autocracy, who turned the country which they had conquered into a battle-field of rival factions.

After the death of Perdiccas, a second and somewhat more successful attempt at a settlement was made in 321 B.C. at the conference of Triparadisus. From this time two great personalities emerge from the confused tangle of contending forces — Seleucus and Antigonus. Seleucus, now satrap of Babylon, was obliged by motives of policy to side with his rival in the struggle against Eumenes, but Antigonus saw in a confederate so indispensable a more than probable rival, and Seleucus only anticipated the fate of Eumenes and Pithon by a providential escape into Egypt with a handful of horse. In 312 B.C., however, we find him back in Babylon, casting about for means to establish an empire whose resources would enable him to meet his great rival in the West. Whither could he better turn than to the East? The clash of arms which reverberated through these unquiet years from end to

end of Asia Minor only awoke distant echoes in the
far eastern frontier. East of the Cophen, Macedonian
influence was steadily on the decline, the generals who
had conquered the East being far too busy with the
task of destroying one another to keep an eye on the
government of the lands which had cost them so much
blood and labour to acquire. Pithon, the ruler of
Sind, had been compelled to vacate his command by
320 B.C. Eudamus, in command of the garrison at
Alexandria-on-Indus, went home (after murdering his
native colleague and collecting all the plunder he could
lay hands on [1]), with a body of troops, to participate in
the scramble for power, in 317 B.C., probably only
anticipating expulsion by voluntary evacuation.[2]

West of the Cophen, Stasanor continued to govern
Bactria, and Oxyartes the province which lies in the
triangle between the Indus and Cophen and the Parapamisus range. The kinsman of Darius even appears
to have sent help to the confederates in the war with
Antigonus, but was allowed to remain unmolested.
Perhaps, on the receipt of the news of the tragic end of
his daughter and grandson, he changed sides, or withdrew from the contest ; his influence, in any case, was
of no weight on either side. In 306 B.C. the peace of
Bactria was once more disturbed. Seleucus entered
the country and demanded its allegiance. We may
imagine that it was given without any prolonged
resistance, as Justin passes over the fact in a single

---

[1] Diodorus, XIX. 4.

[2] ". . . India . . . post mortem Alexandri, veluti cervicibus
jugo servitutis excusso, præfectos eius occiderat. Auctor liber-
tatis Sandracottus fuerat " (Justin, XV. 4).

sentence.[1] But when once more the glint of Macedonian pikes was descried on the winding road descending the Kabul Pass, India was ready to meet her invaders on more equal terms. Chandragupta,[2] the first of the Mauryas, had seized the throne of Magadha, expelling the last of the Nandas, whose weak and unpopular rule had left their kingdom an easy prey to this bold usurper.

Chandragupta had studied in the school of Alexander, and had learnt much from the great general whom he worshipped as a hero of semi-divine powers. What happened in the encounter we do not know. Probably Seleucus recognized the futility of a struggle when he found his opponents in such unexpected strength,[3] particularly in view of his coming in conflict with Antigonus. Terms were concluded satisfactorily to both ; and while Seleucus returned with his forces considerably augmented by Indian elephants and, no doubt, subsidies from Bactria, Chandragupta was allowed to extend his domains up to the edge of the

---

[1] "Principio Babylona cepit ; inde, auctis ex victoria viribus, Bactrianos expugnavit" (Justin, XV. 4). This is condensation with a vengeance.

[2] Sandracottus. "Populum quem ab externa dominatione vindicaverat, ipse servitio premebat." (Justin, loc. cit.).

[3] 600,000 infantry, 30,000 cavalry, and 9,000 elephants (V. A. Smith, Early History of India, p. 117, second edition). But it is unwarranted to talk of Seleucus as "defeated" or "humbled," as Smith does. Our authorities imply nothing of the kind. It was a compromise : Seleucus gave up lands over which he had never been able to exercise a de facto sovereignty in return for a lucrative alliance. The actual terms are disputed. For the pros and cons, see Smith, Appendix G, p. 132, of his History of India.

Parapamisus, probably including in his territory
Arachosia and part of Gedrosia. They were useless to
a ruler engaged in a life and death struggle 2,000 miles
away, and, unlike Bactria, were not valuable for sup-
plying subsidies of men or money to any extent.

At Ipsus (301 B.C.) Antigonus fell, and Asia passed
into the hands of Seleucus. For fifty years we hear
nothing of Bactria. The "rowdy" element, it will be
remembered, had passed out of the land on the death
of Alexander, to find their fate at the swords of Pithon's
troops. The remaining Greeks appeared to have inter-
married with the Iranian populace, and to have settled
down peacefully under the rule of the Greek satrap.
Even in religion a compromise appears to have been
effected, the Greeks recognizing in Anahid of Bactria
their own Artemis or Venus. In 281 B.C. Seleucus
fell by the blow of an assassin, and in the endless and
insensate struggle which ensued between Syria and
Egypt, Bactria seized an obvious opportunity to cast
off a yoke which had become little more than nominal.
Antiochus II. (Theos) succeeded his father (of the
same name) in 260 B.C. He carried on the futile
campaigns against his neighbours, and it was not
long ere the inhabitants of Parthia and Bactria
recognized the folly of paying tribute to a distant
monarch who was incapable of enforcing respect or
obedience.

The details of this great revolt, which wrested from
Syria the fairest jewel of her crown, and established
one of the most remarkable of the many offshoots of
Hellenic colonial enterprise in the heart of Asia, are
somewhat obscure. Bactria had enormously increased

in power with fifty years' almost continuous peace;
and Justin's mention of the "thousand cities" ruled
over by the prefect of Bactria conveys a general notion
of the prosperity of the country. The prefect of
Bactria had furthermore, it seems, acquired a certain
overlordship over the satrap of the country which
afterwards became famous as Parthia.[1] This small
tract of land, comprising chiefly the Tejend watershed,
was quite insignificant[2] when compared with the vast
tracts of Bactria and Sogdiana, but contained a breed
of men antagonistic from every point of view to the
province which claimed their homage—they were non-
Aryan, accustomed to plunder their more civilized
neighbours, and born fighting-men. Their satrap at
the time appears to have been one Andragoras, who
may have succeeded on the death of Stasanor. We
cannot, perhaps, do better than to consider what Justin
(our chief authority) has to say about the revolt which
freed Parthia and Bactria from the Syrian Empire.
"After the death of Antigonus," says Justin,[3] "the
Parthians were under the rule of Seleucus Nicator, and
then under Antiochus and his successors, from whose
great-grandson, Seleucus, they revolted, at the time of
the first Punic war, in the consulship of Lucius
Manilius Vulso and Marcus Attilius Regulus. For
their revolt, the disputes between the brothers Antigonus and Seleucus gave them impunity; for the two

---

[1] I infer this from what Strabo says of Arsaces: "According
to one account, he was a *Bactrian*, who withdrew himself from
the encroachments of Diodotus, and established Parthia as an
independent State" (XI. 9, 3).

[2] κατ' ἀρχὰς μὲν οὖν ἀσθενὴς ἦν (Strabo, XI. 9, 2).

[3] Justin, XLI. 4, 5.

latter were so intent on ousting one another from the throne that they neglected to chastise the revolters. *At the same period, also* Theodotus, governor of 1,000 cities in Bactria, rebelled, and took the kingly title, whereupon the other nations of the East, following his lead, fell away from Macedon too. One Arsaces, a man of uncertain origin but undoubted courage, arose at this period. He was accustomed to make his livelihood as a bandit, and heard a report that Seleucus had been worsted by the Gauls in Asia. Feeling himself safe from interference, Arsaces invaded Parthia with a band of brigands, defeated and killed Andragoras, the governor, and took the reins of Government into his own hands."

This is by far the fullest account of the revolution which we possess, and it is more than usually full of Justin's usual inaccuracies. First of all, what does Justin consider the date of the revolt to have been? He mentions "the Consulship of L. Manilius Vulso and M. Attilius Regulus." This was the year 256 B.C. Supposing, however, that Marcus Attilius is a mistake for Caius Attilius, who was consul with Lucius Manilius Vulso in 250 B.C., the latter date would be that of the revolt,[1] and this agrees with the opinion of later authorities,[2] who place the revolt in "the eleventh year of Antiochus II." What Justin means by going on to refer to the "fraternal war" between Seleucus and Antiochus, or to the "report of a reverse suffered

[1] I follow, with some reservations, Rawlinson's *Sixth Oriental Monarchy*, p. 44, note.

[2] Eusebius, *Chronicle*, II., p. 32 ; Moses of Chorene, *History of Armenia*, II. 1 *fin.*

at the hands of the Gauls," it is difficult to determine.
The "fraternal war" broke out on the death of Antiochus Theos in 246 B.C., between Seleucus Callinicus
and Antiochus Hierax; but if this is the case, why
mention the consuls for the year 250 B.C.? Perhaps
Justin is confusing two separate accounts, and we
may reconstruct the story of the revolt as follows :

In 250 B.C. Diodotus revolted (while Antiochus Theus
was busy with his Egyptian war), and Andragoras as
his vassal followed suit. The revolutions were practically simultaneous,[1] but Bactria set the example. But
the native Parthians cordially hated their rivals and
masters on racial and other grounds, and in the years
between 246 B.C. and 240 B.C. (the reference to the
"reverse at the hands of the Gauls" must refer to
rumours about the battle of Ancyra in 240 B.C.), a
patriotic Parthian, who had taken upon himself the
royal title of Arsaces,[2] returned from exile among the
Parnian Dahæ, of the same race as himself[3] in the
Ochus Valley, whence he had been carrying on a border
war since his banishment and slew Andragoras.[4] He
then proceeded to set up a purely native state, strongly
anti-Hellenic,[5] in which all traces of Alexander's
influence were effaced. This, however, is at best a

---

[1] "*Eodem tempore,* Theodotus——" (Justin, XLI. 4). Strabo
says : πρῶτον μὲν τὴν Βακτριάνην ἀπέστησαν οἱ πεπιστευμένοι,
. . . ἔπειτα ᾿Αρσάκης ἐπῆλθεν καὶ ἐκράτησεν αὐτῆς.

[2] Arsa-kes (*cf.* the Scythian Maua-kes) was a title, not a name,
as Justin remarks (XLI. 5). So Surenas (commander) was often
mistaken for a proper name. *Cf.* Tac., *Ann.*, VI. 42.

[3] Strabo, IX. 9, 2.   [4] Justin, XLI. 5.

[5] The title "Phil-Hellen" assumed by the later Parthian
kings is merely an attempt to repel the taunt of "barbarism"
levelled at the race by its more cultured neighbours.

conjectural version of the story, and takes no account of the assertion of Arrian,[1] that the revolt was against Pherecles, satrap of Antiochus Theus.

It seems fairly clear, however, that Diodotus revolted in the reign of Antiochus Theus, and this theory finds some support in the coins of Bactria which have been handed down to us. In Professor Gardner's *Coins of the Seleucid Kings of Syria*[2] we find figured one series which bears the inscription of Antiochus II., but a portrait which is certainly that of Diodotus, as figured in his coins. Did Diodotus, as Professor Gardner thinks, issue these coins, as a first tentative step towards open rebellion, "to supplant his master in the eyes of the people"? It may well be so, and we may conjecture that he did not venture into open revolt until he found this first advance unreproved by the Syrian monarch.[3]

Other authorities, relying on the fact that the face of the coins is that of a young man, consider the whole series to belong to the younger Diodotus, and that the father issued no coins in his own name at all.[4] In support of this theory, it must be remembered that Diodotus I. appears to have died in 245 B.C. (if we date the change in policy towards Parthia from

[1] Fragment I. Arrian makes out that it was a private quarrel. The satrap grossly insulted Tiridates, whereupon his brother murdered him and raised a rebellion.

[2] Plate V., 7.

[3] For discussion of the whole question of dates in connection with the two revolts, see Rawlinson, *Sixth Oriental Monarchy*, chap. iii.; Bevan, *House of Seleucus*, i., p. 286; and V. A. Smith, *History of India*, p. 196.

[4] V. A. Smith, *Catalogue of Coins in Calcutta Museum*, Introduction and Notes, pp. 6, 7.

his death), and coins would scarcely have the same opportunity of passing into general circulation as they would in the long reign of his son.[1] The Bactrian coins are all particularly fine and interesting, and those of the Diodoti are among the best. The cognizance of the Diodoti, before and after the revolt, appears to have been the figure of " Zeus thundering." Von Sallet puts down to Bactria, before the revolt, the silver coins [2] bearing the bust of Antiochus II. on the reverse, and on the obverse Zeus, striding to the left and hurling a bolt. These may belong to the period of Diodotus I., and the coins mentioned above as bearing the types and names of Antiochus and the portrait of Diodotus may have been the earliest issue of his son. Other fine coins of Diodotus (father or son—the face is always the same, and is that of a young man, clean shaven, with a severe but purely Hellenic type of feature)—are the gold one pictured by Professor Rapson,[3] and the silver ones figured by Gardner in his catalogue.[4] All bear the image of the " Thundering Zeus," striding to the left and hurling his bolt, on the reverse. One bronze coin only bears

[1] In dealing with Euthydemus, we shall observe that he claims "to have destroyed the *children of those who first rebelled.*" This surely implies that Strabo believed in the existence of *two* rulers of the name of Diodotus, the *second* of the two being the one whom Euthydemus murdered. Justin is quite clear on this point : "Tiridates, morte Theodoti metu liberatus, cum filio eius—et ipso Theodoto—fœdus ac pacem fecit."

[2] I.M., 7616 and 9304.

[3] In his article on Greek and Scythian coins contributed to the *Grundriss der Indo-Arischen Philologie.*

Gardner, *Catalogue of Greek and Scythic Kings*, etc. Plate I., Nos. 4 to 8.

a figure of Artemis with torch and hound, and on the obverse a head which may be that of Zeus.[1]

It has been already remarked that there was no love lost between the Bactrians and their fellow-revolters, the Parthians. The Parthians, who immediately followed the lead of their powerful neighbours, did not win complete freedom for some years afterwards, probably, as we have seen, not till after the accession of Seleucus Callinicus; and, apparently, Arsaces dreaded Bactria a good deal more than Syria.

The year 247 B.C. witnessed the meteoric invasion of Syria by Ptolemy Euergetes, who penetrated to the very borders of Bactria, without, however, entering the newly-constructed kingdom, as far as we can judge. The expedition stopped short at this point, owing to domestic sedition, and the invasion of Ptolemy was only one more incident of the cruel and useless war that was draining the life-blood of Western Asia. Tiridates (or Arsaces II., for his brother, the great founder of Parthia, had fallen in battle) now proceeded to annex Hyrcania, and shortly after took the surprising step of coming to terms with Bactria. This effectually disposes of the theory that Diodotus II. only exists in the pages of Trogus and Justin.[2] The alliance could never have been made in the reign of the first Diodotus, the determined opponent of Parthia,

[1] Gardner, *Catalogue of Greek and Scythic Kings*, etc., Plate I., 9. Diodotus assumes the title Σωτήρ, referring (if the title has any definite meaning) to the part played by Bactria in protecting the eastern flank of the Hellenic world from the barbarians. This was always acknowledged to be the chief function of Bactria.

[2] Introduction to Gardner's *Catalogue*.

and the strongest foe to Arsaces, even from motives of fear, for it is not likely that the "prefect of a thousand cities" would fear a discredited and harassed monarch like Seleucus. It is more likely that the treaty was concluded, as Justin says, by the second Diodotus, just before the advance of Seleucus to subdue the invader of Hyrcania, whose challenge could hardly be overlooked. We may conclude, then, that Diodotus II. succeeded his father some time between the acquisition of Hyrcania by Parthia and the invasion of Seleucus. Common consent has fixed the date at about 245 B.C. Diodotus reigned till 230 B.C., and probably lived to regret the unnatural alliance he formed in his early youth, for Tiridates, thanks to his complaisance, won a complete and unexpected victory over the "ever-victorious" Seleucid, and launched Parthia on its great career as the rival, not only of Bactria or Syria, but Rome itself.[1]

Diodotus fell the victim of a court conspiracy, at the hands of one Euthydemus, a Magnesian, who appears to have taken effectual means to prevent any of the rival family from disputing his right to the throne. It is possible that the murder was caused by discontent at the tame policy of Diodotus, who appears to have done little for Bactria in comparison with his successors, and certainly committed a fatal error of policy in his alliance with Parthia. Diodotus appears to have fallen some years before Antiochus III. appeared on the throne of Syria, which was as well for the sake of Bactrian freedom. His death probably

[1] Date uncertain. Rawlinson (*Sixth Oriental Monarchy*, p. 48) says 237 B.C. But is this not too late?

took place about 230 B.C., after which a great change takes place in Bactrian policy, marked by a corresponding cessation of activity by the Parthians.

So ended the dynasty which founded Bactria as a free state. In themselves not remarkable, later monarchs[1] were glad to claim kinship with the earliest kings of Bactria, and even to give Diodotus I. the title of " Divine."

ADDITIONAL NOTE TO CHAPTER IV.

ANTIMACHUS " THEOS " : This mysterious king, whose title would lead us to suppose him to be a personage of some importance, is only known to us from coins; historians have overlooked him. He appears to have been a son, or close relation of, Diodotus II., as his coins bear on the obverse that king's head, and on the reverse the naked Zeus hurling the bolt. V. A. Smith (*Catalogue of Coins in Calcutta Museum*, p. 10) thinks "he succeeded Diodotus II. in Kabul." But surely Kabul was at this time in the hands of the Mauryas.[2]

He appears to have been a member of the royal house, who, on the murder of Diodotus II., proclaimed himself as the rightful heir. The inscription on the coins—ΒΑΣΙΛΕΥΟΝΤΟΣ ΑΝΤΙΜΑΧΟΥ ΘΕΟΥ—is that of a man who wished to emphasize his " divine right " to the throne, and after a brief reign as the head of "the legitimist faction," was quietly crushed by Euthydemus.

---

[1] Agathocles. See his coins in Gardner (Plate IV., and Introduction, pp. xxviii, xxix).

[2] See, however, V. A. Smith, *Early History of India*, p. 194, and Rapson, *Coins of the Andhras*, Introduction, p. xcviii.

AUTHORITIES.

Strabo, XI. 9, 3; Justin, XLI. 4, 5, etc.; V. A. Smith (*Early History of India*), E. R. Bevan (*House of Seleucus*, vol. i.) give accounts of the rebellion. Some useful remarks will be found in Rawlinson's *Sixth Oriental Monarchy*, chap. iii. For coins, see Gardner's *Catalogue of the Coins of Greek and Scythic Kings of Bactria and India in the British Museum*. Valuable articles by Ed. Meyer (*s.v.* Diodotus, Bactria, etc.) will be found in the *Encyclopædia Britannica*, eleventh edition.

CHAPTER V

IT must have been about the year 230 B.C. that Euthydemus, the Magnesian, murdered Diodotus and usurped his throne. Who Euthydemus was is quite unknown ; but no doubt a kingdom with the romantic history of Bactria appealed to the Greek imagination, and attracted many "soldiers of fortune" ready to make a bid for success in the new world which had just been thrown open to them.

The treachery of Euthydemus was palliated, if not justified, by its success. Under him and his successors Bactria not only magnificently vindicated her rights to an independent existence, but launched upon a career of conquest and expansion which paralyzed her rivals, and was destined to spread Hellenic influence more surely and permanently than had been done by the great Macedonian himself. So remarkable is the career of Euthydemus, that later historians forget the existence of Diodotus. "The house of Euthydemus," says Strabo, "was the first to establish Bactrian independence."[1] It is possible, indeed, that

[1] He is thinking of the successful repulse of Antiochus; before this Bactria was only a kingdom "on sufferance."

64

the weak and vacillating policy of Diodotus particularly towards Bactria's national and well-hated rival, Parthia, was to a large degree responsible for his murder, which could hardly have taken place without the connivance of at least the great Iranian nobles.

Euthydemus had some years of uneventful prosperity in which to consolidate the empire he had seized before he was challenged to vindicate his right by the ordeal of war. In 223 B.C. Antiochus III., second son of Seleucus Callinicus, succeeded to the throne of Syria. Antiochus has some right to the title of "The Great," which he assumed. He is one of the few Syrian monarchs for whom we can feel any real respect, combining as he did the personal valour which had become a tradition among the successors of Alexander's generals with a military talent and a reluctance to waste the resources of his kingdom in interminable petty campaigns, which is only too rare in his predecessors.

It was only in reply to a direct challenge from Parthia that Antiochus interfered at all in what was taking place in the east of his dominions. Artabanus I. (who succeeded Tiridates I. about 214 B.C.), pursuing the policy of aggression which under his predecessors had succeeded so admirably, took advantage of the rebellion of a satrap named Achaeus to advance and occupy Media. This was open defiance, and Antiochus could not ignore it if he would. An arduous campaign followed. Antiochus did not make the mistake of underrating his foe, and Justin even puts his forces at 100,000 infantry and 20,000 cavalry.[1] However, the Parthians merely fell back farther and farther into their mountain fastnesses, and at length the dogged courage of Artabanus found its own reward.

The independence for which Parthia had fought so well and so persistently was at last recognized, and Antiochus even condescended to form an alliance with his gallant antagonist,[2] though lesser Media was restored to Syria. Perhaps, however, it was Artabanus who suggested to Antiochus the invasion of the rival State of Bactria, and he may even have lent him troops or promised co-operation. He may have pointed out to Antiochus what was fast becoming apparent, that Bactria, under the peaceful rule of Euthydemus, with its great natural resources, and the advantage of an enterprising Greek to direct its fortunes, was fast becoming a menace to Parthia and Syria alike. Besides, it would be a triumph of diplomacy if Parthia could divert the forces of so dreaded a neighbour against her cherished rival. Whichever way the fortunes of war might veer, Parthia must be the gainer. If Antiochus were successful, the fidelity and assistance of Artabanus might be rewarded by the control of Bactria, and, at the least, Bactrian aggression would be checked for ever. On the other hand, if the Syrian forces were defeated, anarchy would no doubt soon reign once more in Syria, and Parthia would find her opportunity for further expansion once again. Antiochus had an excuse at hand for yielding to the arguments

[1] Justin, XVI. 5.
[2] *Ibid.*, "Postremum in societatem ejus admissus."

of Artabanus, if indeed we are right in supposing the
Syrian monarch to have been influenced in his action
by his new ally.   Bactria had incurred the enmity of
the Seleucids in the reign of the last monarch; the
weak and short-sighted policy of Diodotus II. had
enabled Parthia to establish her independence, as we
have seen, unmolested; and, above all, the Syrian
Empire, rich though it was, had been almost exhausted
by years of suicidal war and misgovernment, and
could ill afford the loss of the most fertile of her
provinces, "the glory of Iran," [1] as it was popularly
called.   To regain the allegiance of Bactria was a
natural ambition.

The expedition against Bactria must have started
in the year 209 B.C., perhaps in the early spring.
Antiochus chose to attack the country by approaching
from the south and striking at the capital.

The campaign has been described by Polybius [2] in
the concise vivid style which gives the reader so ready
an impression of military operations.   Unfortunately,
the chapter is an isolated fragment only, and breaks
off after a description of the battle with which the
campaign opened, leaving all account of the subsequent operations a blank.   Of the invasion, however,
the ravages of time have spared us a minute account.
Antiochus marched along the southern borders of the
Arius, the river which rises in the Hindu-Kush, and
loses itself, like so many rivers in that region, in the
shifting sands and fertile patches just beyond the
Tejend Oasis.   The invader had of necessity to choose

[1] Strabo, *Geog.*, XI. 11, 1.
[2] Polybius, XI. 34, and X. 49.

his route in a march upon Bactria, if he wished to
avoid the hardships and perils of the Bactrian wastes.

He learnt that the ford [1] by which he intended to
cross into the enemy's territory was held in force by
the famous Bactrian cavalry, and to attempt to force
a passage in the face of these was to court disaster.
Knowing, however, that it was a Bactrian custom [2]
to withdraw their main army at night, leaving a thin
screen of pickets to hold the positions occupied,
Antiochus determined on a bold bid for success.
Leaving his infantry behind, he advanced swiftly and
suddenly with a picked body of cavalry, and attacked,
probably at dawn, so unexpectedly, that he carried
the passage almost unopposed, driving the pickets
back upon the main body.   A fierce encounter now
took place between the picked horsemen of Iran and
Syria.   Antiochus, with the recklessness characteristic
of the successors of Alexander and his generals, led
the charge, and after a hand-to-hand combat, in which
he received a sabre-cut in the mouth and lost several
teeth, he had the satisfaction of routing the enemy
completely.   The main Syrian army now came up
and crossed the river.   Euthydemus appears not to
have risked a general engagement, but to have fallen

[1] Close to a city called by Polybius Ταγουρίαν. Von Gutschmid
emends to Τὰ Γαυρίανα. The ford was a little to the west of
the town.

[2] It was also a Parthian habit. The reason was that the
Parthian and Bactrian troops were almost all *mounted*, and a
sudden night attack upon a mounted force would cause horrible
confusion. Hence they always withdrew to a safe distance from
the enemy at night. A Parthian force, for similar reasons,
never marched or attacked at night.

back on his almost impregnable capital. Of the details of the siege we know nothing, but it may be [1] that it is to this blockade that Polybius refers when he says that the " siege of Bactria " was one of the great sieges of history, and a common-place for poet and rhetorician. Time wore on, and still the " City of the Horse " held out. A long absence from home was unsafe for Antiochus, for the Syrian Empire might at any moment break out into one of those incessant rebellions which were the bane of the Seleucid Empire. Both sides, perhaps, were not unready for a compromise, and this was brought about by the good offices of a certain Teleas, a fellow-countryman of Euthydemus, and hence especially suitable for the task. On behalf of the Bactrian prince, he pointed out that it was illogical to cast upon him the blame accruing from the policy of Diodotus II. in forming an alliance with Parthia. In fact, Euthydemus was the enemy of Diodotus, and had merited the gratitude of Antiochus in destroying the "*children of those who first rebelled.*" [2] A still more cogent argument sufficed to convince the king. The Scythian hordes were on the move, and threatening the borders of the Jaxartes like a storm-cloud. Bactria was the outpost of Hellenic civilization, and on its integrity depended the safety of the Syrian

---

[1] Von Gutschmid takes this for granted. This is scarcely justifiable.

[2] *I.e.*, Diodotus, and probably others of the family likely to be in the way. Perhaps "Antimachus Theos" (see appendix to preceding chapter) was one of them. These words seem to be very strongly in favour of the view that there were *two* kings of the name of Diodotus.

empire; and Euthydemus pointed out that to weaken
Bactria would be a fatal step for the cause of Hellas.
" Greece would admittedly lapse into barbarism." [1]

This is the first mention we have of the aggressive
attitude of the tribes beyond the Jaxartes; [2] but the
problem was evidently not a new one to Euthydemus
or to Antiochus. The Seleucid monarch came to the
conclusion that it was to his interest to preserve the
integrity of this great frontier state, which guarded
the roads from India and the north. The terms [3] on
which peace was concluded must have caused intense
chagrin to the Parthian allies of Antiochus.

An alliance, offensive and defensive, [4] was concluded
between the royal houses of Bactria and Syria : this,
of course, included the recognition of the claim by
Euthydemus to the royal title, which was perhaps
granted on condition that he should guard the
Scythian frontier (for it was chiefly on this ground
that the claim had been put forward); the alliance,
moreover, was to be sealed by the betrothal of the
young daughter [5] of Antiochus to Demetrius, the

[1] ἐκβαρβαρωθήσεσθαι τὴν Ελλάδα ὁμολογουμένως. Von Gutschmid makes a curious mistake here. Taking the passive voice,
apparently, for a middle, he says, in his Encyclopædia article,
that Euthydemus " threatened to call in the barbarians and
overrun the country."

[2] Vide Rawlinson, Sixth Oriental Monarchy, p. 58 note.

[3] For terms, vide Polybius, XI. 34, 9-10. For the whole
campaign (except the siege, of which we have been spared no
account except the doubtful reference, Book XXIX.) I have
followed Polybius. See also Bevan, House of Seleucus, II. 23 ;
and Rawlinson, loc. cit. Date of the treaty, ? 208 B.C.

[4] συμμαχία.

[5] Was she the mother of the Laodicé of the coins of
Eucratides ? See Appendix II., p. 152.

gallant prince who had caught the attention of the Seleucid whilst conducting negotiations on behalf of his father in the Syrian camp. Euthydemus may have urged on Antiochus the propriety of recovering that old appanage of Bactria, the satrapy of Paropamisus. The strategic value of the kingdom of Kabul was beyond question; it had been recognized by Alexander, who had placed it in the hands of Oxyartes, who, as we have already seen, probably continued to administer it till, by the weakness or negligence of Seleucus Nicator, it passed back to the hands of Chandragupta Maurya. It was probably in this domain that Antiochus found the Indian princeling Sophagasenas or Subhagasena reigning; who the latter was is quite uncertain. It was conjectured at one time that the name Subhagasena is a title of Jalauka, a son of the great Asoka, who had died in 231 B.C. ;[1] but Jalauka himself is a misty personality, of whom we know little besides the vague, though voluminous, stories of Kashmir tradition.[2] Euthydemus, on behalf of whom the expedition was mainly undertaken, was under the obligation by the terms of the treaty to provide the means for its accomplishment. For a third time (the last for many centuries) the tramp of armies from the far west was heard down the long winding defiles of the historic Khyber.

But the expedition does not appear to have been carried out with the thoroughness which Euthydemus

[1] First suggested by Lassen, *Indische Alterthumskunde*, I think.

[2] *Vide* Smith, *Early History of India*, pp. 171 and 197, 198.

would have liked. It was little more than a demonstration in force. Subhagasena appears to have
yielded very easily, and consented to the payment
of a considerable indemnity and the surrender of
elephants. Antiochus had already been overlong
absent from Syria, and he hastened home by the
Kandahar road, through Arachosia and Carmania.
Androsthenes of Cyzicus was left behind to receive
the sum owing to the Syrian coffers, and to follow
with it later.[1]

Euthydemus figures on several fine coins which
have been recovered; he appears on them as a man
in the prime of life, with a heavy stern face.[2] The
wide area over which his coins are found points to a
considerable extension of the Bactrian domains. An
attempt was probably made in his life-time to annex
those territories which had been ceded to Chandragupta by Seleucus Nicator, and with the break-up of
the Maurya kingdom on the death of Asoka this was
quite feasible. Doubtless Demetrius took a prominent
part in leading his father's armies, and he may have
been associated with him in ruling in the now extensive dominions of Bactria, though it is probably a
mistake to attribute the Indian expedition and the
foundation of Euthydemia to this reign. It is, of
course, unsafe to draw inferences too certainly from
coins, but the coins of Euthydemus[3] have been dis-

---

[1] ? *Circa* 206 B.C.

[2] See the illustration, Gardner, Plate II.

[3] On the obverse we find either a horse (appropriate in the
case of the Bactrian Zari-aspa, the " City of the Horse ") or the
figure of Hercules,

covered, not only in Bactria and Sogdiana,[1] but in Paropamisus (which may have been put under the suzerainty of Bactria by Antiochus), Arachosia, Drangiana, Margiana, and Aria.[2]

Euthydemus may well have looked back upon his career with pride. By sheer ability he had vindicated his right to the crown he had so violently wrested away. The ablest of the Seleucids had come to punish him as a revolting vassal; before he left, the Bactrian, by his dogged valour, had won that monarch's respect and friendship. He was lord of a great, fertile, and important realm; his son had already shown promise as a warrior and statesman; and the latter's wedding with a princess of the proudest of the Hellenic families, whose royal ancestor, the great "Seleucus the Conqueror," second only to Alexander himself, claimed the God Apollo as his father,[3] was a guarantee of lasting peace and friendship with Syria. The hated Parthians were paralyzed for the time by their rival's success, and Bactria must have been growing rich in her position at the confluence of the world's trade routes. Ever since the day when, according to the oft-repeated story, Bindusara sent to request a "supply of wine and a sophist" from his Syrian contemporary, and Chandragupta sent presents of drugs to his father-in-

---

[1] Does this indicate that the Sacæ were kept well in hand in this reign?

[2] "Apollodorus of Artemita says the Greeks (of Bactria) conquered Ariana." If they did, it was probably in this reign or the next (*Geog.*, XI. xi. 1).

[3] Laodice said that Apollo was really the father of her son. See Justin, XV. 4 *q.v.*

law,[1] the growth of luxury in the Greek world, and the establishment of new cities of the type of Alexandria, must have created a great demand for Indian goods. A further proof of the close ties binding India and the West is found in the fact that, twice at least, Greek ambassadors were in residence at the court of the Mauryas, Megasthenes at the court of Chandragupta, and Deimachus at that of Bindusara.[2]

Frequent as must have been the caravans from Kabul to Bactria, others doubtless arrived from the distant Seres of the north-east, for the then novel commodity of silk was in great demand in the luxurious towns of the new and cosmopolitan Hellenic age, of which Alexandria is so typical. The forum of Bactria must have resembled that of Sagala in Menander's days, when traders of every creed and tongue crowded the bazaars, and the innumerable shops were loaded with the most heterogeneous articles—muslin and silk, sweetstuffs, spices, drugs, metal work in brass and silver, and jewels of all kinds.[3] Small wonder that Euthydemus is regarded as the founder of Bactria. Only one storm-cloud marred the otherwise shining prospect, and that was as yet low down on the distant horizon. The barbarians beyond the Jaxartes were still moving uneasily.[4] About the year 190 B.C. the long and

[1] Müller, *Frag. Hist. Græc.*, i. 344, and iv. 421.

[2] Strabo, II. 1, 9.

[3] Milinda-Pañha, *Sacred Books of the East*, XXXV. 3. *Iron* of a superior quality was also an important item in commerce with the Seres.

[4] If we are to believe the Chinese authorities, the first actual occupation of Sogdiana must have been as early as the reign of Eucratides.

eventful reign of Euthydemus came to an end, and
the kingdom passed to a worthy successor in
Demetrius.[1] Whether Demetrius had already begun
his eastern conquests we do not know, but at some
period of his reign Bactria reached the climax of her
prosperity. The ancient citadel of the Iranians was
the capital of a mighty Empire, as the words of
Strabo testify : " The Greeks who occasioned the
revolt (*i.e.*, Euthydemus and his family), owing to
the fertility and advantages of Bactria, became
masters of Ariana and India. . . . These conquests
were achieved partly by Menander and partly by
Demetrius, son of Euthydemus. . . . They overran
not only Pattalene, but the kingdoms of Saraostos
and Sigerdis, which constitute the remainder of the
coast.[2] . . . They extended their empire as far as
the Seres and Phrynoi." Their object, obviously, was
to reach the sea for trading purposes ; a similar
object led them to secure the highroad into China.

The evidence of the coins of Euthydemus (*vide
ante*) seems to point to the occupation of Aria by
that king.[3] Conquests east of Kabul, on the other

---

[1] 190 B.C. was also the year of the great defeat of Antiochus
by the Romans. Perhaps this fresh disaster to the already
harassed Syrian power encouraged Euthydemus and Demetrius
to use their opportunity for invading India.

[2] *Geog.*, XI. xi. 1 : Δημήτριος ὁ Εὐθυδήμου υἱὸς τοῦ Βακτρίων
βασιλέως· οὐ μόνον δὲ τὴν Πατταληνὴν κατέσχεν ἀλλὰ καὶ τῆς
ἄλλης παραλίας τήν τε τεσσαριόστου (?) καλουμένην καὶ τὴν
Σιγέρτιδος βασίλειαν, etc.

[3] *Demetrius in Anarchosia. Vide* Isidorus Characensis, 19, in
Müller, *Frag. Georg. Græc. Min.*, vol. i., 1855. When was this
town founded? In the reign of Demetrius, or in that of his father?
Probably Aria and Anarchosia were subdued simultaneously.

hand, appear from Strabo's words to have been the work of Demetrius, probably after his father's death, though this is not certain. Strabo speaks very vaguely of the extent of the dominions of Demetrius. By Pattalene he appears to mean the kingdom of Sind, the country which was first taken from Musicanus by Alexander the Great. On the west of the Indus, all the country from the Cophen to the mountains appears to have thus belonged to Bactria; east of the Indus, after the annexation of the kingdom of the Delta (Pattalene), it was not a great step to proceed to subdue the neighbouring kingdom of Kathiawar or Surashtra (the Greek Saraostos). What quite is indicated by the "kingdom of Sigerdis" it appears to be impossible to determine. It may have been some minute "kingdom" (*i.e.*, the domain of some petty raja) between Pattala and Surashtra.

Besides these kingdoms on the coast, we have evidence to confirm the opinion that a considerable portion of the Panjab fell into the hands of Demetrius as well. It is usual to ascribe to him the foundation of the town of Euthydemia, which he named after his father, according to a not uncommon practice. Euthydemia became the capital of the Bactrian kingdom east of the Indus, and under its Indian name, Sagala, grew to be a flourishing city of great wealth and magnitude. The question of the identity of Sagala (or Sakala) is a matter of dispute.[1]

---

[1] Σάγαλα ἡ καὶ Εὐθυμηδία, says Ptolemy. See McCrindle's learned note (*Ancient India*, p. 37). He places it in the Pândya country, west of the Hydraotes, about sixty miles from Lahore. There also appears to have been a town called Demetria in Sind (p. 158).

It is now held that it is not to be confused with the
"Sangala" razed to the ground by Alexander; and
modern authorities identify it with either Shorkot,
near the modern Jhang, not far from the confluence
of the Acesines and Hydraotes, or Sialkot, further
north, near Lahore, and not far from the head waters
of the Acesines.[1] Later on we shall see that
Menander was born "near Alexandria," "200 leagues
from Sagala," and this would certainly point to
Sialkot rather than Shorkot, if "Alexandria" is the
town at the "junction of the Acesines and Indus"
mentioned by Arrian (*Anab.*, VI. 5). It is difficult
to believe that the Bactrians had any permanent
hold on the country up to the Chinese borderland.[2]
Perhaps all that Strabo means is that all the territory
up to the great emporium on the extreme west of
Serike—*i.e.*, Tashkurghan in Sarikol, was under
Bactrian influence, and, perhaps for commercial
reasons, was protected by their troops from the raids
of Sakas and other nomadic marauders.

The coins of Demetrius illustrate the history of
his reign in an interesting manner. Like his father,
he seems to have adopted the god Hercules as his
patron deity, and Hercules figures upon the coins of
Euthydemus and Demetrius,[3] very much as the
thundering Zeus figures on those of the Diodoti, or
the Dioscuri on the coinage of Demetrius's antagonist
and successor, the pro-Syrian Eucratides. These

---

[1] Smith, *Early History of India*, p. 68, note.

[2] See Stein, *Sand-buried Cities of Khotan*, p. 72.

[3] *Vide* Gardner, *Catalogue of Coins of Greek and Scythian
Kings*, etc., Plate II. 9 and III. 3; *vide* note 17 *ante*.

coins were doubtless issued for circulation in Bactria proper, like the famous and striking specimen which Gardner reproduces,[1] on which a figure, almost certainly to be identified as the Bactrian Anahid, appears, clad as she is described in the Zend-Avesta.

For use in his domains beyond the Paropamisus, Demetrius issued a series of coins of a more suitable character, remarkable alike for their workmanship and as representing the earliest attempt at that amalgamation of Greek technique and Indian form, which is one of the most striking features of the coinage of the Indo-Bactrian dynasties.[2] To this series we may safely assign the silver coins which represent the King as an Indian raja, wearing an elephant helmet, and those bearing an elephant's head; these coins are, it must be observed, purely Greek in standard and pattern, and are probably earlier than the series of *square* coins, where an attempt at compromise between Greek and Indian methods first appears.[3]

It seems probable that Demetrius divided his Indian possessions into minor principalities for greater convenience of government. A system of satrapies, or small feudal states, appears to have been the only form of administration found possible by the invaders of India, whether Scythian, Parthian, or Greek. It was, indeed, the form of government most adapted to the eastern temperament. From time to time the

[1] *Catalogue*, III. 1.   [2] *Ibid.*, II. 9 and III. 3.
[3] Illustrated by E. J. Rapson in the *Grundriss*, i. 10; Gardner, XXX. 3. The inscription is still Greek, but a Kharoshthi inscription appears on the reverse. Notice the gradual de-Hellenization, well illustrated by the coinage.

influence of some master mind had consolidated a great empire in India; but the bonds had always been purely artificial, liable to dissolution on the appearance of a weak or incapable ruler. It had become apparent on the death of Asoka how little even the great Mauryas had succeeded in introducing elements of cohesion into their vast and heterogeneous realms.

The small satrapy appears to have been the natural political unit in India, as the city state was in Greece. However, Demetrius did not arrive at a satisfactory solution of the problem of simultaneously governing two distant and diverse kingdoms. Perhaps his continued absence in India aroused the jealousy of the Græco-Iranian kingdom in the north; it may be that the inhabitants of Bactria looked upon Sagala with jealous eyes, as a new and alien capital; at any rate, the absence of Demetrius gave ample opportunity for a rival to establish himself securely in Bactria before the arrival of troops from the far south to overthrow him.

The rival who did this was one Eucratides. Who he was, or what may have been his motive, we can only infer from his coins in a somewhat conjectural fashion; one thing, however, seems more or less plain, that he was connected in some way to the royal house of Seleucus. In his sympathies, and probably by birth, he is distinctly closely bound up with the reigning dynasty in Syria.

Justin implies that he seized the throne about the time of the accession of Mithradates I. in Parthia— i.e., about 174 B.C., or a little earlier. We may suppose that Demetrius was engaged in his Indian con-

quests and the administrative and other problems
they entailed, and either had no leisure to attend to
what was happening in Bactria, or did not feel himself strong enough to march against so powerful a
rival until his power in the south was sufficiently
consolidated. Meanwhile Eucratides was pursuing
a vigorous policy in the north, not always with the
success he deserved. Enemies were springing up in
all directions to menace Bactria, and Eucratides had
to vindicate his right to the throne he had claimed.[1]
The first and most formidable rival was Mithradates I.
Mithradates appears to have succeeded with the
special mission of counteracting Bactrian influence,
for Phraates, his brother, had left the throne to him
in preference to his numerous sons, as the ablest
successor, and one most likely to continue the great
mission of extending Parthian dominion in the east,
the progress of which had been thwarted since 206
B.C., when Antiochus the Great had raised her rival
to the position of ally and equal. The continual
threats of aggression from the Parthians, the ever-
increasing pressure on the frontier, which caused
various wars (perhaps not of great magnitude, but
harassing, as a foretaste of what was to come) on the
Sogdian frontier, and a campaign—against whom
we are not informed—in Drangiana, made the life
of Eucratides anything but peaceful. The struggle
with the monarch he had dispossessed, moreover,

---

[1] Perhaps Demetrius had left Eucratides in charge of Bactria
as Regent. Someone must have been so left; and this would
account for the latter's accumulation of power, his command
in frontier wars, etc.

was coming, and Eucratides went to meet it with great spirit. At one time the fortunes of war seemed to have definitely turned against him; by a final effort Demetrius, with the huge force of 60,000 men, caught and besieged his rival, whose army by some means had sunk to only 300 men. By a marvellous combination of skill and good - fortune, Eucratides cut his way out after a siege, which (if we are to believe the only authority upon the incident)[1] lasted five months, and this proved to be the turning-point in the war. Soon after the Indian dominions of Demetrius fell into the hands of Eucratides, and the once powerful Demetrius either perished or was deposed about the year 160 B.C.

If, as is just possible, Eucratides was really the grandson of his royal opponent,[2] the great disparity between their ages would account for the ease with which that once doughty leader allowed himself to be defeated by a handful of desperate men, whom he had conquered with a vastly superior force; it would also save the historian from the necessity of condemning Justin's whole account of these incidents as exaggerated and inaccurate—always a pre-eminently unscientific proceeding in the case of an uncontroverted statement. The victory over Demetrius is probably commemorated in the fine coins repro-

---

[1] Justin (XLI. 6) tells the story : " Though much reduced by losses (in frontier wars), Eucratides, when besieged by Demetrius, King of India, with a garrison of 300 men only, kept at bay a blockading force of 60,000 of the enemy by continual sorties. Finally, after a five months' siege, he escaped."

[2] See Appendix II., p. 153.

duced by Gardner,[1] which represent, in a most
spirited fashion, "the great twin brethren," with
their lances at the charge, waving the palms of
victory. These were evidently struck for use in
Bactria ; for use in the provinces beyond the Hindu-
Kush very probably he struck a series of coins,[2] where
the blending of Greek and Indian art is illustrated in
a curious manner, bearing the goddess Nikê, holding
a wreath on the obverse, and a Pali inscription on
the reverse, in Kharoshthi[3] characters. The coins are
bronze and square, this being another instance in
which the Indian shape replaces the Greek circular
coin.

It is extremely interesting to notice the manner
in which the Greek temperament adapts itself to
changed conditions. Eucratides gives himself the
title of "Maharaja"[4] (which he translates by the

[1] *Vide Catalogue*, Plate V. 6-9.

[2] *Ibid.*, Plate VI. 6 and 7.

[3] *Kharoshthi* was the script, probably of Aramaic origin, in
use during our period on the west and north-west frontier—Paropamisus, Kapisa, and the Panjab. From here it spread, with
the Buddhist religion, to Khotan, as is shown by the Karosthi
MSS. brought from that country by Sir Aurel Stein. *Brahmi*,
on the other hand, is the original of the Devanagri, used, in one
form or another, in all the modern Prakrit vernaculars. As
most Bactrian coins were minted on the western border, only
a few (issued by Pantaleon and Agathocles) bear Brahmi
inscriptions. Demetrius, one of the greatest of the Bactrian
coiners, was the first to adopt the significant practice of striking
bilingual coins.

[4] *Raja* seems equivalent to *Chhatrapa* (satrap), merely, the
one being used by the native Indian or Bactrio-Indian petty
rulers, the latter, apparently, by the feudatories of Parthia.
To render ΒΑΣΙΛΕΥΣ "Maharaja" is required. The ΜΕΓΑΣ

Greek ΜΕΓΑΛΟΥ ΒΑΣΙΛΕΩΣ) in his Indian
domains; in Bactria, however, he appears as the
leader of the Greek, as opposed to the Iranian section
of the populace. By birth and leanings it seems
evident that Eucratides was thoroughly Greek. His
coins betray his pride of birth; the distinctive figure
on nearly all his Bactrian issues is a representation
of the Dioscuri, mounted; they were the patron saints
of the Seleucids, and under the rule of the "son of
Laodice," took the same place on his coinage as
Zeus, the thunder-god, did on the coins of the
Diodoti. One of the most striking features of Bactria
is the utter predominance of everything Greek in its
history. The coins are essentially Greek, the rulers
are certainly so. The Iranian population never seems
to have had any voice at all in the government,
though we must remember that Greek was the
language of commerce and civilization in Western
Asia, and we are apt to be easily misled by the fact
that Greek names, coinage, and language were exclu-
sively used. In Parthia, for instance, we know that
national feeling was utterly anti-Hellenic, and yet
Greek appears to have been the language generally
used for commercial and public purposes. Perhaps
it was his partiality for Greek customs and his pride
in his Seleucid blood that brought about the downfall
of Eucratides.

ΒΑΣΙΛΕΥΣ of some of the coins is an attempt at a "literal"
translation of "Maharaja." *Chhatrapa* was a title probably
introduced into India from the Parthians. Some critics have
(wrongly, I think) seen in this word traces of Persian influence
on Indian political development (see Chapter VIII.). σατραπης
τῶν σατράπων first appears on the coins of Mithradates I.

While returning from India, Justin tells us, he was murdered by his own son, who had shared the throne with him, and who, far from concealing the murder, declared that he had killed " not a parent, but a public enemy," and brutally drove his chariot through the dead monarch's blood, and ordered his body to be cast out unburied (*circa* 156 B.C.). Thus perished one of the most remarkable of the many really great, though obscure, monarchs of the Bactrian Empire. A splendid coin, figured by Gardner in his catalogue,[1] enables us to form a very good idea of the appearance of the king—a proud, determined man, wearing the *Kausia*,[2] diademed with crest, and the bull's horn at the side. On the reverse, significantly, are figured the Dioscuri, charging with long lances and waving the palms of victory. The delineation of the steeds is worthy of the highest traditions of Greek Art. The title of ' *the Great* ' appears on the coin, ΒΑΣΙΛΕΩΣ ΜΕΓΑΛΟΥ ΕΥΚΡΑΤΙΔΟΥ.[3] The name of the parricide who thus foully deprived his father of his life and throne is not recorded. Some authorities have identified him with Heliocles,[4] who

[1] Gardner, Plate V. 7.

[2] See p. 102, *n*.

[3] Another coin of this reign is the magnificent twenty-stater gold piece, at present in the Bibliothèque Nationale at Paris. It was, as far as we know, by far the largest gold coin struck in antiquity (Alexander issued two-stater pieces), and is in every way unique. It fittingly marks the high-water mark of Bactrian prosperity under Eucratides; after this reign it gradually decayed. After the reign of Eucratides only silver and copper coins were struck, as far as we know.

[4] Tarn, " Hellenism in Bactria," *J.H.S.*, 1902, p. 272.

is supposed by them to have headed a native reaction, fomented either by his father's Hellenizing tendencies, or by his inactive policy against Mithridates. Mithradates, we know, took the satrapies of " Aspionus and Turiva "[1] from Eucratides, and it is possible that this caused dissatisfaction at the policy of the Bactrian monarch. There is, however, some reason to suppose that the parricide's name was Apollodotus,[2] who may have been led by the supposed patriotic character of his deed to assume the titles of ΣΩΤΗΡ, ΝΙΚΗΦΟΡΟΣ, and ΜΕΓΑΣ,[3] which we find on his coins. It is supposed that Heliocles avenged his father's murder and secured the throne, probably putting his brother to death; some have thought that this is indicated by the title "ΔΙΚΑΙΟΣ," which appears on his coins. It is probable, however, that the title of the "Just" is of Buddhist origin, but this point may be more appropriately discussed later on.

Apollodotus seems to have enjoyed a very brief reign, and Heliocles probably succeeded in 156 B.C. With him the rule of the Greeks in Bactria comes to an end; the Bactrian princes were forced to transfer

---

[1] Strabo, *Geog.*, XI. ii. 3. Nothing more is known of them. The names are Iranian. Lassen thinks they are Turan and the Aspaciacæ.

[2] Cunningham, *Num. Chron.*, 1869, p. 241, etc. See, however, *J.R.A.S.*, 1905, p. 783. If Apollodotus succeeded Eucratides, why does Eucratides restrike his coins, as he is shown to do by Gardner, *B.M. Cat.*, p. xxxv? On the other hand, Apollodotus is closely connected with Menander. See p. 112.

[3] It has been pointed out that the titles Σώτηρ, Νικήφορος, 'Ανίκητος, and the like, point to the continual wars against the nomads, Indians, or their Greek rivals, which drained the resources of the Bactrio-Hellenic princes.

their empire to their capital beyond the Hindu-Kush. The murder of Eucratides was worse than a crime—it was a blunder. The death of the one man capable of saving the situation rendered resistance useless, and the country was still further enfeebled by the rise of a number of princelings or satraps, who were necessary for the government, as we have seen, of the immensely increased Bactrian territory, but who were always inclined, on the removal of a strong hand, to assert their independence. The semi-independent character of these petty rajas[1] is shown by the style of the inscriptions upon their coins.

AUTHORITIES.

Justin and Strabo, among ancient writers, are of the most importance. The works of Messrs. E. R. Bevan and Vincent Smith are the principal modern authorities. The writers on numismatics are, of course, invaluable, as much of Bactrian history is "deduced" from coins, which eke out our otherwise scanty information. For a further discussion of the coins of Eucratides see Appendix II.

---

[1] There are nearly thirty of them. See the lists, pp. 151, 152.

CHAPTER VI

SINCE the days when Alexander made his demonstration in force north of the Jaxartes, and the town of Furthest Alexandria, built on the uttermost limit of the Greek world, was erected as a frontier fort to keep watch and ward over the barbarians of the outer waste, there had been a feeling of vague unrest among the Greeks in the Far East regarding the likelihood of trouble from the mysterious hordes of the northern steppes.

No one knew their extent or power, which made them all the more formidable. Perhaps memories of the terrible Cimmerians of the old days had become a kind of tradition in men's minds, for at all periods of the history of the ancient world we seem to detect a feeling of latent anxiety, a prescience of what was to come, with regard to the vast tribes of " barbarians " who from time to time burst like a sudden cyclonic wave on the barriers of civilization—feared, because their numbers, power, and resources were only known through vague report and extravagant rumour. The very fact that the Parthians, once an obscure nomadic tribe, pasturing their herds on the grassy slopes between the Oxus and the Ochus, had suddenly thrust

into the heart of the Greek world a great anti-Hellenic
empire, proud of its antagonism to Greek ideas, and
aggressively eager to dispute with all comers its right
to the position of ruling state in Asiatic Greece, was a
warning of what the barbarians might do, and of the
risk of despising him.[1]

Bactria was destined to be overwhelmed by the
operation of the same irresistible force which finally
swept the civilization of the ancient world utterly
away. Obscure hordes on the Mongolian plains, far
beyond the ken of Hellenic observation, were slowly
but surely pressing south, and the impetus was finally
being transmitted to the tribes on the fringe of Hellenic
civilization, till at last, by sheer physical pressure,
they were driven over the border, sweeping all before
them with the force of an avalanche.

Signs of trouble on the northern border had been
observed by Euthydemus, and Antiochus the Great
had had the wisdom to see the danger of weakening
Bactria. Other causes, however, had been at work to
drain Bactria of her resources : the constant antagonism of Parthia, and the brilliant but expensive conquests of Demetrius in India, till at last the Bactrian
Greeks were literally " drained of their life-blood," as
Justin graphically says,[2] "and a comparatively easy
prey." Indeed, one of the most striking features of

---

[1] In Chapter I. I have tried to point out the likelihood of
a *Sacæan Helot population* in Bactria—an aboriginal substratum, whose existence points to the constant tendency of the
northern tribes to move southwards and westwards, which had
begun before the coming of the Iranians.

[2] *Exsangues*, XLI. 6.

Bactrian history is the wonderful persistence of the Greek element. No Iranian ruled in Bactria after the accession of Diodotus, and the Greek kings, if we may judge by their coins, were proud of their Hellenic blood, and kept up the best traditions of their national art. Even in the Southern Kingdom there appears at first little evidence that the new-comers were likely to be absorbed into their Indian environment; on the contrary, few things are more remarkable than the manner in which the Greek spirit adapts itself to altered circumstances, and blossoms out into a new life, infusing something of the "diviner air" of the old masters into the coins of Menander and his contemporaries, or, later, into the friezes of the Buddhist sculptures of Gandhara.

In the troubled times which followed the death of Eucratides events occurred which must have finally wrecked any chance Bactria had of offering any effectual resistance to the impending invasion of the Sacæ. Heliocles, as we have seen, succeeded Eucratides. We know very little of him except that his coins invariably bear the inscription $\Delta IKAIO\Sigma$. It was formerly held that he murdered his father and took this title to assert the justice of slaying a king whom a section of his subjects appear to have regarded as a public enemy. It is more probable, however, that Heliocles was his father's avenger, and on that ground assumed the title of the "Just," though the title may merely be a translation of the Buddhist dhârmikasa, if, indeed, Heliocles was influenced by the spread of Buddhism to the extent to which most of his successors appear to have been.

Mithradates, as we have noticed already, had inaugurated the aggressive policy against Bactria, for which he had received his crown in the reign of Eucratides, with some success. If, as it has been asserted, Eucratides lost his life owing to his inability to resist Parthian aggression, his successors were not less deserving of a similar fate.[1] Mithradates continued to advance, and he appears to have actually held Bactria for a time as a sort of vassalage. If we can trust references in Orosius and Diodorus, he even attacked the Southern Kingdom, and penetrated to Euthydemia itself. We may fairly safely infer, however, from the silence of Justin, and also from the fact that no Parthian coins are found over the Paropamisus, that the occupation was not of a very lasting character, and may indeed have only been a demonstration in force, like the expedition of Antiochus III. against Subhagasena.[2] Perhaps we may find an echo of these obscure and almost unrecorded campaigns in a Parthian coin which is still extant in the British Museum collection.[3] It represents a standing figure of Hercules, and appears to have been imitated from the coins of Euthydemus II. and Demetrius of Bactria.[4]

Fortune, however, appears to have intervened on this occasion on behalf of Bactria. Demetrius II. of Syria had not quite forgotten the claims which Bactria

[1] Perhaps the murder of Eucratides, caused by popular indignation at his " pro-Parthian " policy, was a kind of challenge to Mithradates, which he was not slow to accept.

[2] He appears to have subdued the Saka Princes of Taxila, the kingdom between the Indus and Hydaspes.

[3] Catalogued by Warwick Wroth, Plate III. 7.

[4] Gardner, *Catalogue*, II. 9 and III. 3.

had on the Seleucid house—claims arising from the
treaty of Antiochus, and the ties of marriage uniting
the two royal families. Between the years 142—136
B.C., he advanced against Parthia, intent on another
of the many spasmodic efforts of the Syrian kings to
check the growth of their powerful rivals. His army
on the march was greatly strengthened by reinforce-
ments from Persia, Elymais and Bactria, and routed
the Parthians in a succession of battles.[1] The Parthians, however, maintained the struggle with their
usual persistency, and finally achieved by stratagem
what they were unable to effect by force. Demetrius
was enticed to his enemy's camp by pretended overtures and entrapped. He was publicly paraded as a
warning to the cities which had joined his standard of
the futility of reliance upon Syria.

In the year 136 B.C. Mithradates I. died. He was
succeeded by Phraates II., and it was during his reign
that the great Saka invasion took place, which
swept over Bactria with such amazing suddenness
and completeness. The movements which led to the
great irruption have been worked out with tolerable
completeness, chiefly by reference to Chinese authorities; however, it is not proposed here to enter into
minute discussions upon the obscure movements of
the various tribes, with the many historical difficulties
they involve, as the subject is scarcely relevant to the
student of the fortunes of Bactria, and only interests
us in so far as Bactria is directly concerned. What
happened appears to have been as follows:

About the year 165 B.C. the great tribe of the

[1] Justin, XXVIII. i. 3, 4.

Yuehchi were driven out of their pastures in North-West China by a rival horde, and, moving in a south-westerly direction, came into contact with the con-glomerate bands of Scythians, whom the Greeks knew by the vague general name of Sacæ, who may be identified pretty certainly with the Saka of the Indian writers, and the Su, Sai, Se, Sek, or Sok, of the Chinese Annalists. The Sacæ appear to have already settled to some extent south of the Jaxartes; we know nothing for certain about the state of Sogdiana under the Bactrian kings, but probably, with the extension of the empire in the south, the Greek hold on the province north of the Oxus became more and more nominal, till it was finally no longer asserted at all.[1]

About the year 136 B.C., after the death of Mithra-dates, the results of this pressure upon the Bactrians and Parthians began to be seriously felt. The first omen of the approaching trouble proceeded from a body of Sacæ who had enlisted as mercenaries in the army of Phraates, probably because they had been driven out of their old pasture-lands and had no other occupa-tion. They arrived too late to assist in the war for which they were hired, and, being discontented at the treat-ment they received, began to plunder the country. Phraates, who appears to have been incapable and unpopular, fell in trying to put them down, chiefly owing to the treachery of his Greek forces, who were exasperated by his cruelty.[2]

The Parthians now reverted to the original royal line

[1] See the passage (b), Appendix V., p. 163, "Bactriani . . . Sogdianorum bellis fatigati," etc.

[2] Justin, XLII. 1, 2.

for a successor to the throne, whom they found in
another brother of the elder Phraates, Artabanus, uncle
of the last king. Artabanus appears to have followed
these plunderers up; but in a campaign against the
Thogarii, says Justin, he was wounded in the arm and
died at once — possibly because the weapon was
poisoned. One is strongly tempted to identify these
"Thogarii" with the "Tochari," who, together with
the "Asii, Pasiani, and Sacarauli,"[1] are mentioned by
Strabo as being the best known of the Sacæan tribes
who crossed the Jaxartes and invaded Bactria. The
Tochari appear to have established themselves on a
more or less permanent footing in Sogdiana, and so
would naturally be the chief opponents of the Parthians.
The Sacæ appear to have exacted tribute in a most
extortionate manner from the people bordering on the
country they had overrun, forcing them to pay a certain
sum of money on condition that their lands should
only be overrun and plundered at certain seasons.[2]

To Heliocles belongs the melancholy distinction of
being the last king of Northern Bactria. The Bactrians
were, indeed, little in a fit state to cope with the situation.
Their life-blood had been drained by the Indian schemes
of preceding kings, and the consequent withdrawal of
the more able and adventurous among them to seek a
more extended career in the new addition to the
empire; and, as in the case of every nation which has
tried to conquer the East without taking the utmost
precaution to preserve the integrity of their race from

---

[1] *Geog.*, XI. 8, 2. Von Gutschmid thinks *all* these names
attempt to render "Yuei-Chi" in Greek.

[2] Strabo, *Geog.*, XI. viii. 3.

intermixing with the subject stock, the East was gradually absorbing them into itself. As we have already observed, the coins begin to show that Greek standards of thought and manners were gradually becoming less and less carefully adhered to; and an account of the state of Bactria, presumably shortly after the invasion of the Sacæ, confirms the view that Bactria had little that was Greek left in it at the time of its final overthrow. From the annals of Chang-Kien[1] we learn that the Ta-Hia, or Bactrians, were very like the other tribes between Ferghana and An-Si (Parthia). These people all spoke various dialects, but all understood one another; they were agricultural, treated their wives with an exaggerated respect, and allowed them great liberty, and were all distinguished by deep-set eyes and thick beards. They were bad and cowardly soldiers, and only fond of trade.[2] The description of the Bactrians here given by one who was evidently a close and accurate observer shows fairly conclusively to what extent the process of absorption had been going on, and explains what would be otherwise difficult to comprehend—the reason why Bactria succumbed without a struggle worth recording to the incoming flood of invasion. Two brief references are

[1] Envoy from the Chinese Court to the Yueh-Chi. He returned, after various adventures, in 126 B.C.

[2] Von Gutschmid says it is "remarkable that Chang notices no difference between the Greeks and their Iranian subjects." The explanation is simple : there were no pure Greeks left. Some remains of the old Aryan (Iranian, not Greek) population may still be traced in the language of the non-Tartar people dwelling round Balkh (Rawlinson, *Herodotus*, App., Book VII., Essay 1, p. 207 ; M. Müller, *Languages of the Seat of War*, p. 33).

all that western historians have deigned to devote to
the subject, and the inference is that the once famous
"City of the Horse" surrendered tamely enough to
the advance of a foe so long threatened that it had
lost the terror of novelty. Heliocles and such families
as had enough Greek instinct to refuse to dwell under
the rule of the illiterate barbarians probably retired
before the enemy's advance to their friends on the.
other side of the Paropamisus. It was far different in
the case of the once weaker Parthia, which was able,
not only to repair the losses suffered from the Scythian
attack, but finally to retake part of the old Bactrian
territory ;[1] so that the poet Horace—with some inaccuracy, it is true, can write

"*Regnata Parthis Bactra,*"

in an ode which must have been published about the
year 25 B.C.

The barbarian invasion, then, may be said to have
branched off into two distinct channels. The motive
force was provided by the advance of the Yueh-Chi ;
and this great movement, which ended by the Yueh-Chi
occupying the old kingdom of Bactria, forced another
great portion of the Sacæ—the Sakas proper, possibly
the Sok or Sse of our Chinese authorities, and the
Saca-rauli of Strabo — to seek "pastures new" still
farther from the borders of their restless and powerful
kinsmen. This no doubt caused the Saka irruption

---

[1] I have not thought it necessary to discuss Bayer's theory
that the Greeks were driven out of Bactria by *Parthia*. He
misunderstands Strabo. Strabo tells us that Mithradates II.
and his troops ἀφείλοντο τῆς Βακτριανῆς μέρος, βιασάμενοι τοὺς
Σκύθας (XI. 9, 2).

into India, though how and when the Saka princes
found their way into the Panjab is never likely to be
definitely settled. It is usually supposed that they
descended into the Ki-pin or Cashmere Valley, and
from thence gradually spread over the Gandhara district, and finally settled in a series of petty principalities in the Panjab, such as the very flourishing states
of Taxila and Mathura (the modern Muttra), on the
Jumna, from which they displaced native rajahs.
Others even reached the Peninsula of Surasthra,
across the formidable Sind deserts, and, together with
the Greek invaders already settled in the north-western
corner of India, inaugurated a period which has left
behind it some very remarkable traces, both in coinage
and architectural remains. There was no contemporary
historian to chronicle the brief careers and brilliant
courts of the Rajas of Taxila or Sagala ; it remains for
us to read the riddle, as far as may be, from the
evidence which the ravages of time have spared for
the ingenuity of the modern investigator.

We have seen that Euthydemus hoped to manage
his huge realm upon a kind of feudal plan, which had
obtained from immemorial time in the East. Probably
one of the earliest of the princes who reigned south of
the Paropamisus was another Euthydemus, whom it is
convenient to call Euthydemus II. He appears to have
been a son of Demetrius, and named, according to the
old Greek custom, after his grandfather. His reign, to
judge by the paucity of coins, was short. It is probable
that he was reigning in the Kabul Valley, while two
other princes, Pantaleon and Agathocles, were holding
small frontier kingdoms on the west bank of the Indus.

It is curious to note that, while the coins of Euthydemus II. indicate that he ruled over a people who had a good deal of Greek blood in their veins, those of his two contemporaries are much less Hellenic in character. These two princes issued some remarkable nickel coins, and also some square copper ones bearing inscriptions in the Brahmi,[1] instead of the usual Kharoshthi script. Their general similarity in these respects, and also the fact that both put the bust of Dionysius on their coins, make it seem highly probable that the two princes were closely related in some way. Pantaleon appears from his portraits to have been the older, and probably Agathocles succeeded him. Pantaleon and Euthydemus were probably contemporaries, and date from some time fairly early in the reign of Demetrius, soon after that king had begun to attempt some definite settlement of his newly-acquired domains in the south. We shall probably not go far wrong in dating their accession at *circa* 190 B.C., and that of Agathocles at about five years later.

With Agathocles we get numismatic evidence of a rather startling quality, in the shape of a magnificent series of medals which that monarch struck, apparently on his accession. Nothing is more remarkable than the manner in which the Greek spirit flashes out in all sorts of unexpected ways in sculptures and coins of these scanty remnants of the great invasion, a couple of centuries after it had flowed over the Kabul and re-

---

[1] *Brahmi script.* See note in previous chapter. The Brahmi script was used in India proper, the Kharoshthi being confined to the "foreign" population of the western frontier, where it was probably introduced by Darius. Kharoshthi, unlike Brahmi, reads from right to left.

ceded again. A petty Yavana Raja, with little, probably,
of the Greek blood he boasted in his veins, and perhaps
but little acquaintance with the tongue of which he is
so proud, can strike medals which have a Hellenic grace
which would not shame the best traditions of Greek
art, and which, with a curious pride of race, assert
the striker's kinship with the heroic founders of the
Bactrian kingdom, and the Seleucid monarch who was
glad to be their friend and ally. The first of the series[1]
is that bearing the portrait of the great Alexander
"Son of Philip" himself; then comes Diodotus, the
founder of the Bactrian Empire, with the title ΣΩΤΗΡ,
which appears on one of that monarch's own coins;
Euthydemus I.[2] with the title ΘΕΟΣ—ancestor, no
doubt, of the monarch; and, lastly, Antiochus Nicator.
The latter, it appears, must be none other than
Antiochus III., whose daughter married Demetrius.
Agathocles is proud of his descent from the royal line
of Bactria. Would he not naturally be far prouder of
his connection with the Seleucids, the family which, in
spite of two centuries of blundering and misrule, still
enjoyed a semi-divine reverence from their subjects,
descended, as they claimed to be, from Apollo himself?
Gardner and other authorities[3] hold that the very title
Nicator is against the identification of Antiochus with
Antiochus III., who assumes invariably on his extant
coins the title of ΒΑΣΙΛΕΥΣ ΜΕΓΑΣ. However,

[1] Figured in Gardner's *Catalogue*, IV. 1-3. They trace this
descent back to Philip of Macedon, doubtless to impress the
subjects with their monarch's importance.

[2] Notice the royal fillets and title ΒΑΣΙΛΕΥΣ.

[3] Gardner's *Catalogue*, Introduction, pp. xxxviii, xxxix;
Babelon, *Rois de Syrie*, XLII.

Gardner himself, quoting "from a passage of Malala,"[1] admits that the title appears to have been actually used by Antiochus III., and certainly he would appear most appropriately on Bactrian coins. These coins bear on the reverse the striding Zeus, already familiar to us as the crest of the Diodoti. Two curious coins throw some side-lights upon the policy and tendencies of the smaller Bactrian principalities. On a coin of Pantaleon appears a spirited representation of a nautch girl, wearing trousers, and depicted as dancing, with a flower in her hair. Whether this was an attempt to conciliate his Indian subjects, or to commemorate a court favourite, it is impossible for us to tell.[2] The vivid delineation of a typically eastern subject with something of the grace of the Greek is another landmark in the history of the Hellenic race in one phase of their absorption into the country they had invaded. More remarkable in many respects is the purely Buddhist coin (IV. 10, Gardner), where the Stupa or Dâgaba, and the Buddhist Rail are delineated.

There is no doubt that Buddhism took a strong hold on the invaders of India from the north-west— indeed, the Panjab and the Gandhara district appear to have become the centre of Buddhism in its palmiest days. Two of the most remarkable of the kings of that part of India, the Greek Menander and the Scythian Kaniska, were Buddhists, the latter ranking

---

[1] John of Malala, the Byzantine, i., p. 261. Why *should* Antiochus II. appear on Bactrian coins?

[2] Agathocles issues the same type. Probably there is no personal reference in these types; they belong to different districts, of which they are the crest or symbol. See Rapson, *Coins of the Andhras*, Intro., p. xi.

next to Asoka himself in the history of the creed of Gautama. The reason is not far to seek. The invaders, quickly settling in the land of their adoption, had none of the prejudices, the conscious desire for isolation, which creates so infinite a gulf between rulers and ruled in the East of to-day; they were ready to adopt the customs and gods of the country, to worship, as the precept of Socrates enjoined, "after the fashion of the state they dwelt in." But orthodox Brahmanism had no place for the "barbarian," the foreign casteless chieftain, who might enter their cities, but seldom their ranks; Buddhism, on the other hand, had none of the exclusiveness of the Brahmin creed; it boasted, on the contrary, of its disregard of caste, and hence, when partly displaced in India proper by Brahman influence, it retained its hold on the Scythian and Greek invaders, and spread to far countries like Ceylon and Japan, and even to the fastnesses of Thibet.[1]

Contemporary, or nearly contemporary, with these princes appears to have been Antimachus Nicephorus —Antimachus II., as he is usually called, to distinguish him from the mysterious prince of that name who appears to have been a rival of Euthydemus when the latter overthrew Diodotus, and to have claimed in some way to be the rightful successor to the throne of the murdered king. It would, then, seem that

[1] This is not quite correct. A recent inscription (*J.R.A.S.*, 1909, p. 1092) tells us of the Greek Heliodorus, son of Dion, a subject of Antialcidas, who was a votary of Krishna-Vasudeva. But Buddhism is, on the whole, far more cosmopolitan, and more likely to make foreign converts.

Euthydemus distributed his eastern domains among members of his family, probably reserving the capital, Sâgala, for himself and his direct descendants, such as Demetrius, who had actually undertaken the conquest of the East. Among the other princes of the house of Euthydemus was Strato I. The figure of the sedent Hercules upon his coins indicates his relationship to that monarch.[1] It seems probable that Strato I. was a son of Euthydemus by Agathocleia, and that the widow acted as regent during his minority.[2] One coin has been discovered which apparently bears a portrait of the queen-mother.[3] He was a contemporary of Heliocles, and was succeeded by Strato II., apparently his grandson. Coins of Heliocles, of the Persian standard, square and with bi-lingual inscriptions, are found in the Kabul Valley, and were probably issued after his expulsion from Bactria by the Scythians.

Among this confused mass of petty princes, whose coins are the only evidence for their existence, it is possible to trace out here and there two distinct lines of succession—the feudatories who claimed descent from Euthydemus, and those who based their royal right upon their loyalty to, or kinsmanship with, the usurper Eucratides. To the former group belong

[1] Compare Gardner's representation, XI. 6, with the Euthydemus type, I. 11.

[2] An interesting discussion of the coins of Strato I. and Strato II., by Professor Rapson, will be found in the *J.R.A.S.*, 1905, p. 164. Also *Corolla Numismatica* (Oxford, 1906), p. 245. The identification of Gardner's coin (XI. 2) is due to him ; Gardner says it is a head of Apollo. But notice the Indian queue, or hair-knot. [3] Gardner, XI. 2.

Pantaleon, Agathocles, Antimachus II., Strato, and his descendant of the same name;[1] to the latter, Antialcidas,[2] Lysias, and Diomedes. Their coins, except one, bearing the figure of an elephant, figured by Gardner (*Catalogue*, VII. 9), are all bi-lingual, and show unmistakable signs of deterioration from the artistic point of view; they seem to be the work of artists to whom Greek tradition is little more than a meaningless form, and are mostly bad copies of the Dioscuri type of Eucratides.

The frequent recurrence of the Dioscuri on these coins leads to the opinion that the princes who struck them wished to intimate their association with the house of Eucratides. Lysias, too, appears wearing the "Kausia," or highland bonnet, which was, as we have already mentioned, affected by Eucratides.[3] Perhaps Plato, whose coin dates itself at 165 B.C., was the first of this line. To proceed farther, however, with the list of minor rulers of whose achievements even their coins can teach us little, is useless to all practical purposes; it is now necessary to turn to the history of those Saka chieftains who were settled side by side with the Greeks in the Panjab and the surrounding districts. In all probability they had entered India from the north, as already related, passing through the country of the Byltai (little Thibet), into Ki-pin, or Cashmere, and thence down

---

[1] Also Menander, if we may judge by his adoption of the styls of Demetrius. See next chapter.

[2] Antialcidas is perhaps the only Græco-Bactrian king mentioned in contemporary inscriptions. See Appendix, from which we learn that his headquarters was Taxila.

[3] Gardner, XI. 7. Kausia, a "sun hat" ($\chi\alpha\upsilon\sigma\acute{\iota}\alpha$), first introduced into the East by the Macedonians. *Vide* p. 84.

the Indus. The Saka who entered India are no doubt those Sai-Wang (princes of the Sai) whose defeat is mentioned in the ninth chapter of the Han annals.[1] Even before this one body of the Saka had settled in the valley of the Cophen, which they found an easy conquest, owing to the raid of Mithradates I. (*circa* 160 B.C.). Two important cities became the centres of Saka rule. The first (and doubtless the oldest, situated as it was in the country into which the Saka first entered) was the town of Taxila, on the Cashmere borderland; the second, far inland, was the great city of Mathura, or Muttra, on the Ganges, between which and the other Saka states lay various hostile principalities, Greek and Indian. The earliest of the satraps of Mathura of whose date we have any clue appears to have been a certain Rajavula, whose later coins appear to imitate those of Strato II. This would enable us to fix his date roughly at about the year 120 B.C. Now, Rajavula succeeded two satraps, Hagana and Hagamasha, whose predecessors appear to have been native Indians, to judge by their names; hence we feel justified in placing the occupation of Mathura at about a generation before the accession of Rajavula. Mathura was very probably occupied at a later date than Taxila,[2] although coins give us no support in

---

[1] Bühler, *Ep. Ind.*, i. 36. Also inscription "*P*" from Lion Capital.

[2] Taxila (Takshasila) was in the dominion of Antialcidas (inscription quoted on previous page). Takshasila was a very ancient centre of Buddhist learning—a kind of "University town." For the Saka satraps see Rapson, *Coins of the Andhras*, Intro., p. ci.

this view, the first known satrap of Taxila being the Liaka Kusuluka of the "Taxila grant,"—the inscription engraved on a metal plate, which has been found in the neighbourhood of the modern city. The Saka are also mentioned (unless the reference is to "Sakya,"—*i.e.*, Sakya-muni, a title of the Buddha), in an inscription at Mathura, commonly dated at about 100 B.C., or earlier.

The most remarkable, and from many aspects inexplicable, fact is that these "satraps," as their very title implies, are subordinate in some way to Parthia. The only explanation that can be offered is that the Sakas were in occupation of the Taxila country somewhat earlier than the time when we first find traces of their settlement there, and that Mithradates in his Indian expedition actually annexed the old kingdom of Porus, as von Gutschmid infers.[1] "The Kingdom of Porus" included the nations between the Indus and the Hydaspes, and would also include the princes of Taxila, who had henceforth to be content with the title of "satrap," which it is improbable they would otherwise assume, it being the custom with their neighbours to assume a style, the grandeur of which appears to be in inverse proportion to the size of the petty realms they governed. Mithradates appears to have exacted from them an allegiance, which was, however, more or less nominal, as there are no traces of a permanent Parthian occupation south of the Hindu-Kush, and Justin[2]

[1] From Orosius, V. 4, and Diod. Sic., p. 597.
[2] XLI. 6. "He extended the Parthian Empire from the Euphrates to Mount Caucasus," *i.e.*, the Paropanisus.

expressly names this range of mountains as the limit of his kingdom to the East.

Probably this invasion of India took place soon after the death of Eucratides, and, with the death of the great Parthian monarch himself, no doubt the hold of Parthia on the Saka princedoms became more and more a nominal matter, till about the year 120 B.C., or perhaps some twenty years later, a very remarkable personage, whom we may conveniently call by the name of Moga, established himself as an independent monarch at Mathura, and assumed the overlordship of the Saka kingdoms of the Panjab and the Kabul Valley. He assumes the very title which their former overlord Mithradates had vaunted, that of "Great King of Kings," and appears to have been looked upon as the founder of a new era.[1] The copper-plate inscription from Taxila shows that the rulers of that principality willingly acknowledged the overlordship of Moga. "Patika, son of the Chatrapa Liaka Kusuluka," it reads, "re-enshrined a relic of Buddha, the Stupa of which was in ruins . . . in the seventy-eighth[2] year, of the fifth day of the month Panemus, of the Maharaja Moga the Great (Maharajasa Mahantasa

---

[1] See Fleet's articles, *J.R.A.S.*, 1905, p. 155, and October, 1907; also V. A. Smith, *J.R.A.S.*, 1903, pp. 46-58; F. W. Thomas, *J.R.A.S.B.B.*, 1906. The date of Maues is fixed by Dr. Bhandarkar at A.D. 154, *J.B.Br.R.A.S.*, 20, p. 292 *ff.* For Maua-Kes compare Arsa-Kes.

[2] It is almost certain that the seventy-eighth year of (the era of) Moga is 99 B.C. Notice that Moga uses a Macedonian month (Πάνημος = Μεταγειτνιων in the Attic calendar). Here we see Parthian influence at work.

Mogasa)." No coins, however, of this "great" king
have been found bearing the name Moga; this would
be in itself a very remarkable fact, but the difficulty
is solved by identifying Moga with the Maues or
Mauas (we only know the name in its genitive form
MAYOY[1]), of whose coins we have a considerable
number. That the Saka name Mauakes was well
known, and held by the chiefs of the race at one
period at least, we know from Arrian, where we find
that a leader of that name commanded the Saka contingent of archers at Gaugamela. Recent researches
have proved that—Kes is a common " Kose-suffix,"
and is frequent in the form-Gas. Hence Mo-ga, or
Maua-kes, is very probably the Mauas, or Maua, of
the coins; and, indeed, it would be extremely difficult
to account for many circumstances (particularly the
total absence of coins of "Moga *the Great*," amid the
many specimens of minor princes which have come
down to us) on any other hypothesis.

In the meantime the Greek kingdoms were engaged
in numberless petty wars. Very seldom does the same
name appear twice, and never more than twice, in
the coins of these petty rulers; and from the dates,
as far as we can determine them, it appears that
frequent and often violent changes in the succession
took place with great frequency. No less than twenty-
three names occur in the space of a century—the
century after the conquests of Eucratides—and an
Indian authority speaks of the "fiercely-fighting
Yavanas," and mentions that "there was cruelly
dreadful war among them; they did not stay in

---

[1] Kharoshthi *Moasa.*

Madhyadesa."[1] An echo of some forgotten war, perhaps against a Greek neighbour, perhaps against the Saka hordes, is commemorated in a brilliant series of coins of Antimachus (Gardner, V. 1-3), in which Poseidon is figured with the palm of victory. Antimachus had won some naval victory, possibly fought on the broad Indus, with a rival flotilla, striving to effect a landing with troops in his domains. One great king, however, arose, whose power was sufficient to enable him to knit together the warring states into something like a consistent whole; his brilliance, piety, and valour are recorded in brief scraps of information which testify in themselves to his power, for he is the only Greek king of the period who has left a mark upon contemporary literature at all. This was Menander, to whom we shall devote the succeeding chapter. Menander appears to have not only consolidated the Greeks into something like a coherent mass, but to have pushed the Scythians of Taxila and Mathura back to the bounds of their original domains, while the mysterious Saka settlements of Surashtra and the lower Indus—an independent branch of the nation, an overflow, perhaps, of the settlers in Sacastene, quite separate from the tribes who entered from the north—were apparently subdued altogether.[2]

---

[1] *Gargi-sanhita*, ed. Kern, p. 57. The word "Yavana" is the Sanskrit form ; Yona the Prakrit. "Yavana" must date from times when the digamma was still in use (Ἰάϝων). Perhaps they were first known in India through Darius the Great. So "Javan" in Isaiah lxvi. 19.

[2] It is, however, not ascertained whether the Saka reached Kathiawar till after the reign of Menander.

The stupendous achievements of Menander, however, were only a transitory flash of brightness in the slowly settling gloom, which was gradually overtaking the Indo-Greek peoples.

AUTHORITIES.

Principally the coins, and the books treating of them. References, even in Justin, our chief authority, are very scanty. The reason probably is that there was very little to relate of these petty semi-Greek rajas, who did little but maintain incessant struggles and issue coins, whose magniloquent inscriptions are strikingly at variance with the insignificant princelings they commemorate. I may add with regard to the names "Moga" and "Moa," that Prof. Rapson regards both as merely dialectical variants of the same word. Moa-kes would become "Moaga," not "Moga."

CHAPTER VII

MENANDER TO THE EXTINCTION OF GREEK RULE IN THE EAST

MENANDER, the Milinda of the Buddhist records,[1] is the only Bactrian king after Eucratides of whom contemporary history really tells us anything. The reason is not far to seek. Of the other Greek princes of the Panjab there is simply nothing to record. Amid the stirring events of the Middle East historians naturally neglected the doings of these petty rulers maintaining a precarious existence on the banks of the distant Indus, and ruling a few square miles of barren desert. The pretentious titles assumed by these insignificant potentates—$\Sigma\omega\tau\acute{\eta}\rho$, $\text{'}A\nu\acute{\iota}\kappa\eta\tau\sigma\varsigma$, and the like—afford no clue to their real importance, though in many cases they bear eloquent testimony to the struggle for existence going on continuously among the Greeks themselves, and against Saka, Parthian, and Hindu invaders. The coins of these princes are really only important in so far as they show us how persistently the artistic instinct of the Greek survived, even in the most un-

[1] The identity of Menander and the Pali Milinda may be accepted. Dr. Rhys Davids identifies Milinda's Yavana courtiers, Devamantiya and Anantakaya, as Demetrius and Antiochus.

109

promising surroundings. Indian writers dismiss the "Yavanas" with the contemptuous epithets of "quarrelsome," or "viciously valiant," which sufficiently indicates their character and the nature of their achievements—such as they were.

However, with Menander, the last of the great Bactrian monarchs, and the only one after the Greeks crossed the Hindu-Kush to show constructive ability, we come to deal with a different type of character. Menander was a worthy successor of his forerunners, Euthydemus and Eucratides, and echoes of his achievements even reached the distant West, and found a place in the pages of Greek and Roman historians. In the East, too, the increased activity of the Yavanas brought them more and more into contact with their Hindu neighbours, and from more than one Indian source we gather records of conflicts and other evidence of the expansion of the Indo-Greek Empire under this enterprising ruler. But the most curious and interesting evidence bearing on the reign of Menander is to be sought, not in historical records at all, but in a Buddhist philosophical dialogue, the *Questions of Milinda*, which sets forth the teaching of the so-called "southern" Buddhist school in the form of a series of conversations between the Buddhist sage Nagasena and the Greek king. There is a good deal of difference of opinion about the historical value of this book. The actual dialogues are, of course, as imaginary as the conversations of Socrates in the works of Plato, and its English translator, Dr. Rhys Davids, even thinks that the evidence for the conversion of Menander to Buddhism at all is inconclusive. But this is going too far.

Apart from the great antecedent probability that the Greeks should be involved in the spread of Buddhism among the foreign settlers of the Panjab and the North-West Frontier, we have the evidence of the coins, conclusive enough when taken in conjunction with other facts—notably, the Siamese tradition of Menander's attainment to Arhatship,[1] and the story preserved by Plutarch of Menander's obsequies, which are just such as would be accorded to a great Buddhist monarch. Menander's coins, like those of Agathocles,[2] often bear Buddhist symbols, such as the *dharma-chakra*, or "Wheel of the Law,"[3] and many of the square bilingual ones bear the significant Pali epithet "DHRAMIKASA,"[4]—"follower of the *dharma*"—which appears to be a Buddhist epithet. It must be stated, however, that the term *dhármika* may be merely a "literal" translation of the Greek epithet ΔΙΚΑΙΟΥ, which appears on the obverse, just as the epithets *trâtârasa* and the like are used by Menander and other kings, Greek and Indian, as the equivalent of the title ΣΩΤΗΡΟΣ.[5] Dr. Rhys Davids declares that the

---

[1] The Arhat is a saint who has attained the supreme spiritual insight which leads to Nirvana (extinction of desire) and consequent escape from future rebirth.

[2] A Buddhist *stupa*, or cairn, and the "rail," a very common decorative feature in Buddhist architecture (see Gardner, IV. 10).

[3] Gardner, XII. 7. The "wheel" is a favourite Buddhist symbol—originally Vishnaivite—signifying the progress of the *dharma*, or religion, of Gautama over the world. For the favourite character of this emblem see Cunningham, *Coins of Ancient India*, p. 101, etc.

[4] Gardner, p. 50, No. 74, and Wilson, *Ar. Antiq.*, p. 287, No. 16.

[5] The question is briefly this: Is *dhramikasa* a translation

bulk of the coins are "clearly pagan, not Buddhist." Probability and evidence, however, appear to combine in pointing to the truth of the story of Menander's conversion. It is likely, too, that the *Questions of Menander* contains a good deal of actual fact in its historical setting. The book was written very likely not later than a century and a half after the great monarch's death, and, as the internal evidence clearly shows, in the Panjab, where the author would be able to become acquainted with traditions, if not actual documents, relating to the reign of the famous Greek raja who reigned so widely in North-Western India.

Menander was probably born about the year 180 B.C., soon after Pushyamitra Sunga had usurped the throne of the Mauryas, and begun to drive the holders of Buddhist tenets into the foreign dominions of the Panjab, by reversing the liberal policy of his unorthodox predecessors. Owing to this Brahminical reaction, the pro-Hellenic tendencies which had distinguished the court of Magadha under its late rulers[1] were discontinued, and a sharp dividing-line was drawn between the foreign settlers of the North-West and the orthodox kings of the Middle Land—the Ganges Valley and the adjacent country.

The coins of many of the later Greek kings show that, if not converted to Buddhism themselves, they ruled over Buddhist subjects. Buddhism eagerly

---

of ΔΙΚΑΙΟΥ, or *vice versa?* But it does not affect the main question—the inherent probability that Menander became a Buddhist. The epithet occurs on the coins of about ten Indo-Greek and Indo-Scythian kings altogether.

[1] Not so pronounced, however, after the death of Asoka.

sought for Greek and other foreign converts, and
recently discovered inscriptions show that Greeks were
even admitted to Hindu sects.[1]

About 190 B.C., it will be remembered, Demetrius first
descended upon the Panjab, and, profiting by the respite
resulting from the Roman invasion of Syria, had seized
the opportunity of overrunning and annexing a great
kingdom in North-Western India. Probably Menander
was a near relation of Demetrius.[2] His coins show a
striking resemblance to those issued by that monarch,
and it was in the Indian territory which he reconquered
for the Greeks that the future prince, who so closely
resembled him in military prowess, was born. " In
what district were you born, O King ?" asks Nagasena
of Milinda, in the *Questions*. " There is an island
called Alasanda," replies Milinda; " there I was born."
" And how far is Alasanda from here (Sâgala) ?"
" About 200 *yojanas*." . . . " In what town, O King,

[1] Appendix III.

[2] Menander's name twice occurs in conjunction with that of
Apollodotus, who is supposed to be the grandson of Demetrius.
Perhaps the two kings were closely related. The passages are
remarkable, as they indicate that Apollodotus was a man of some
ability. He apparently carried on his father's Indian conquests,
and his coins had a wide circulation. They are as follows :

(*a*) "Deinde . . . Scythicæ gentes, Sarancæ et Asiani, Bactra
occupaverunt et Sogdianos. Indicæ quoque res additæ, gestæ
per Apollodotum (MSS. Apollodorum) et Menandrum, reges
eorum " (Trogus ap. Justin., Prologue, lxxi.).

(*b*) Ἀφ᾽ οὗ μέχρι νῦν ἐν Βαρυγάζοις παλαιαὶ προχωροῦσι δράχμαι,
γράμμασιν Ἑλληνικοῖς ἐγκεχαραγμέναι ἐπίσημα τῶν μετ᾽ Ἀλεξάν-
δρον βεβασιλευκότων Ἀπολλοδότου καὶ Μενάνδρου " (*Periplus*,
chap. xlvii.).

Apollodotus is nowhere else mentioned except in these two
passages. See p. 85.

8

were you born ?" " There is a village called Kalasi,"
answers the king; "it was there I was born." Unfortunately, the details here given do not help us very
much. Taking the Buddhist yojana even at its lowest
computation of, roughly, four and a half miles,[1] it
seems quite impossible to find any place 900 miles from
Sialkot, Shorkot, or Chuniot, (all of which have been
identified with the ancient Sâgala), which can possibly
fit this description. Very likely the author is merely
writing loosely, and has greatly exaggerated the distance. The " Island of Alasanda " may be any one
of the numerous islands which dot the course of the
lower Indus. Alexander's activity in this part of India
was immense,[2] and a string of forts, towns, and trading
centres extended along the Acesines, and down to the
mouth of the Indus. Owing to the constant changes
in the topography of the stream, it is now hopeless to
try and discover the actual island referred to—the
scene, no doubt, of some forgotten exploit of Alexander.
Possibly it stood at the juncture of the Acesines and
Indus, and took its name from the great city of Alexandria on Indus,[3] which stood there, not far from the
modern Utch. This town may have given its name to
the neighbouring islands. It was strategically of great
importance, and had been left by Alexander on his re-

[1] So Fleet, *J.R.A.S.*, 1906, p. 1012. Rhys Davids says seven
miles, which would make the " Island of Alasanda," 1,400
miles from Sâgala, somewhere in the Indian Ocean !

[2] Some of the cities in the Panjab, Sind, and Kabul were
Alexandria under Caucasus, which guarded the road to Bactria ;
Nicæa on the Jhelum ; Bucephala on the Acesines ; and many
others, including Alexandria on Indus, mentioned below.

[3] Arrian, *Anab.*, VI. 14, 15.

treat with a strong Greek garrison. Its commandant, Eudamus, withdrew his men during the general evacuation of India in 317 B.C., and the town remained in Indian hands until reconquered by Demetrius. It then, presumably, remained a part of the Greek dominions till the general downfall of the Indo-Greeks after the death of Menander. Its celebrity appears to have spread to distant lands. The *Mahavamso*, the chronicle of the kings of Ceylon, speaks of "Alesadda of the Yonas," referring, no doubt, to this great stronghold of their Greek co-religionists. We hear nothing more of the "town of Kalasi," standing on this island. Formerly it was identified with a supposed Karisi of a coin of Eucratides, but this identification has been since abandoned.[1]

One of the many puzzling problems connected with Menander is that of ascertaining the probable limits of his reign. Von Gutschmid fixes the dates as approximately from 125-90 B.C., inferring this from the "lack of unity" of the Saka coins, which he attributes to the disturbing influence of the Greek invasion. Menander, however, can scarcely have been a contemporary of the powerful Saka monarchs, Maues and Azes, who were reigning in Taxila and Mathura between 100-50 B.C. The rise of the Sakas must have taken place after the Greeks had dwindled into insignificance. Maues would certainly have been an obstacle in the way of the Greek conquests. His rule extended as far as Kipin, while Azes appears to

---

[1] See the introduction to Rhys Davids' translation of the *Questions*. Professor Rapson now reads Kavisa—*i.e.*, Kapisa, Kipin, North-East Afghanistan—on the coin in question (Appendix II.).

have been even more prosperous, if we may judge by the number of his coins which have been recovered. It is also more probable that the independent Saka[1] kingdoms came into existence after the death of Mithradates I. During his reign they appear to have been under the overlordship of Parthia, probably as a result of his invasion of India. On many grounds, then, it appears to be most reasonable to suppose that the great expansion of Greek power took place *before* the foundation of the Saka Empire of Taxila, which could only possibly have arisen after Menander's death, when the "Yavanas" had once more begun to decline. The overthrow of both the Saka and Greek kingdoms was due to the advance of the Kushans, who finally absorbed both alike. We are therefore justified in supposing that Menander was previous to Maues. His great invasion of India is referred to by Patanjali, who appears to have written about 150 B.C.; and he seems to have come in contact with Pushyamitra Sunga, the usurping general who seized the throne of the Maurya dynasty about 184 B.C. Hence we may roughly suppose that Menander reigned at Sâgala from about 165-130 B.C.,[2] and was a contemporary of Mithradates I.[3]

[1] I have used the word "Saka" to indicate the line of kings from Azes to Gondophares, to whom Mr. V. A. Smith gives the title of Indo-Parthian. Personally, I do not think they were Parthian at all, and were only vassals of Parthia for a brief period.

[2] The passage quoted from the *Periplus* (p. 112) makes Menander a contemporary of Apollodotus (acc. 156 B.C.), and connects both with the period of the Scythian invasion of Bactria (160-130 B.C.).

[3] There is no reason to suppose that Mithradates I. and

The capital of the Indo-Greek Empire was the fortress of Sâgala, very probably to be identified with the modern Sialkot. An interesting and vivid picture of this distant outpost of Greek civilization is given in the *Questions*. Its wealth of detail seems to point to an historical foundation to the description. "There is in the country of the Yônakas a great centre of trade, a city that is called Sâgala, situated in a delightful country well watered and hilly, abounding in parks and gardens and groves and lakes and tanks, a paradise of rivers and mountains and woods. Wise architects have laid it out, and its people know of no oppression, since all their enemies and adversaries have been put down. Brave is its defence, with many and various strong towers and ramparts, with superb gates and entrance archways, and with the royal citadel in its midst, white-walled and deeply moated. Well laid out are its streets, squares, cross-roads, and market-places. Well displayed are the innumerable sorts of costly merchandise with which its shops are filled. It is richly adorned with hundreds of alms-halls of various kinds,

---

Menander came into collision. Mithradates had (probably in the reign of Heliocles) penetrated as far as the Hydaspes, and had forced the Saka satraps to do him homage. But the expedition was only a military demonstration (so unimportant that Justin does not mention it), and Parthia, unlike Bactria, wisely confined herself to affairs north of the Hindu-Kush. Hence Menander's conquests provoked no opposition from Mithradates and his successors, who had their hands already full. In the same way, I infer that Menander and the great Saka monarchs could hardly have been contemporaries, or else one would have quickly crushed out the other. But Menander's campaigns were against Magadha, not against the Sakas.

and splendid with hundreds of thousands of magnificent mansions, which rise aloft like the mountainpeaks of the Himalayas. Its streets are filled with elephants, horses, carriages, and foot-passengers, and crowded by men of all sorts and conditions—Brahmins, nobles, artificers, and servants. They resound with cries of welcome to the teachers of every creed, and the city is the resort of the leading men of each of the different sects. Shops are there for the sale of Benares muslin, of Kotumbara stuffs, and of other cloths of various kinds; and sweet odours are exhaled. from the bazaars, where all sorts of flowers and perfumes are tastefully set out. Jewels are there in plenty, and guilds of traders in all sorts of finery display their goods in the bazaars which face all quarters of the sky."[1]

This description exaggerates, no doubt, the wealth of Sâgala, but it at any rate preserves a valuable tradition of the splendour of the Greek capital. As we should expect, it is described as an opulent trading centre, like the parent city of Bactra, where east and west travellers from Europe, Alexandria, China, and India, met to barter; and the writer refers in an interesting way to the proverbial eagerness for knowledge of the Greek, with his " cries of welcome to

[1] *Sacred Books of the East*, vol. xxv., pp. 2, 3. It is possible that memories of Menander and Sâgala inspired the wonderful descriptions of the royal city of Kusâvatî and its king. Maha. Sudassana, " a king of kings, a righteous man who ruled in righteousness, an anointed Kshatriya," in the *Maha Sudassana Sutta (Sacred Books of the East,* vol. xi.). Such stock descriptions of the Ideal City are, however, not uncommon in Buddhist and Jain literature.

teachers of every creed." The author of the *Questions* certainly preserves a tradition of the phenomenal prosperity of the Bactrian Greeks of his day, and constant references are made to their high social status among their Hindu contemporaries. "Wifes of Yonakas, nobles, and Brahmins," are classed together as "delicate women" in more than one passage. Evidently the "Yonaka " was no barbarian, but had secured a high rank in Indian society. It is not known, of course, when the Milinda embraced Buddhism, but the evidence of the coins, and the flourishing state of his capital at the time, seems to indicate that he was already a great conqueror, ruling over a far larger empire than his immediate predecessors. Perhaps we may suppose the conversion to have taken place after his conquest of Western India, but prior to his expedition into the Gangetic plain. A realistic touch is added to the account of the coming of the Buddhist mission to Sâgala ; the writer describes the monks as they flitted to and fro among the white Ionic pillars of the citadel of the great Indo-Greek, glistening in the tropical sun, as "lighting up the city with their yellow robes like lamps, and bringing down upon it the breezes from the heights where the sages dwell."

Probably the earliest of Menander's achievements was to recover the Indian domains of Demetrius, and Strabo refers to an account given by Apollodorus of Artemita of this.[1]

---

[1] *Geog.*, XI. xi., § 1 : "The chiefs of Bactria conquered more territory in India than Alexander. . . . They (*i.e.*, Demetrius and Menander) got possession not only of Pattalene (Sind), but

This involved, no doubt, a campaign against the numerous Greek and Saka princelings of the Panjab, who were forced to acknowledge the overlordship of Sâgala, the latter probably transferring to Menander their allegiance (more or less nominal) as " satraps " of Parthia. The most important of Menander's early undertakings was the reduction of Pattalene and Sigerdis (the coast-line from Karachi to the Gulf of Kachh), and of the solitary Saka settlement of Surashtra (the Kathiawar coast). Another campaign to the north led to the annexation of Kapisa and territory on the borders of Khotan, in the regions of the Mongolian " Seres and Phrynoi." The object of these expeditions was not merely the acquisition of fresh territory ; by the extension of his power to the north Menander secured the important trade with China, while he followed Alexander's plan of conquering the tribes along the Indus bank and at the mouth of the river for similar commercial reasons. The possession of a seaport is always indispensable to industrial prosperity, and the trade between the mouth of the Indus and the Persian Gulf had been considerable since the days of Darius I. The result of this wise policy is visible in the opulence of Sâgala, referred to in the passage of the *Questions* already quoted.

Mithradates I., Menander's only serious rival in the west, was fully occupied by internal reform and

---

of the kingdoms of Saraostos and Sigerdis and the rest of the coast-line (of Sind). Apollodorus calls Bactria the ornament of the Arian land. They extended their empire to the Seres and Phrynoi."

frontier troubles. With the Scythians on the one hand and the Syrians on the other, he wisely resisted the temptation to prosecute further conquests beyond the Hindu-Kush. On the other hand, the great Saka kingdom, which became so powerful in the next generation, had not yet arisen. The scattered Saka tribes, shaken by the invasion of Mithradates, to whom they had sworn a more or less nominal allegiance, remained in a semi-independent condition, an easy prey to a conqueror.

A harder task, however, awaited Menander in Central and Eastern India. Pushyamitra, the commander-in-chief of the Mauryas, had already been nearly thirty years at the head of the kingdom which he had wrested from the degenerate successors of the great Chandragupta. During this time he had considerably restored the ancient glories of the kingdom of Pataliputra, which, though less extensive, was more compact than in the days of Asoka. Its frontier forts on the south lined the banks of the Narmada ;[1] on the west it was bounded by the Saka satrapy of Mathura. Bhilsa, where the king's son ruled as viceroy, was probably the frontier town of the south-west border. It appears to have been about the year 155 B.C. that Menander determined to invade the great kingdom of the west, and try to emulate the achievement of Asoka in conquering the whole of Northern Hindustan. His motive was partly a religious one. Pushyamitra had deserted Buddhism for the older religion of his ances-

---

[1] The Nerbudda, which is usually taken to be the Madâkin of the *Malavikagnimitra* (see V. A. Smith, *Hist. India*, chap. viii., note 3).

tors, and made his kingdom the rallying-point of a great Brahminical revival. With all the zeal of a recent convert, Menander must have been inspired with a desire to restore the ancient ascendancy of the creed of Gautama in the Middle Land, and the proselytizing character of Buddhism naturally accentuated that desire. Pushyamitra, if he had not actually persecuted or insulted the Buddhists, had driven them out of Central India.

On the other hand, Menander's advance was viewed with apprehension by the orthodox subjects of the Sunga monarch. The *Gargî-samhitâ*, in a remarkable passage, gives utterance to their forebodings : " When the viciously valiant Yavanas, after reducing Saketa, the Panchala country, and Mathura reach the royal seat at Pataliputra, the kingdom will be reduced to chaos."[1]

A curious reference to an early encounter between the advancing Greeks and the Indian monarch occurs in the historical drama, the *Malavikagnimitra*. Pushyamitra, who was now an old man, had determined to mark the completion of his conquest of Central India (and, incidently, his utter renunciation of Buddhist principles) by a revival of the ancient Brahminical ceremony of the " horse sacrifice," the *Asva-medha*. The ceremony consisted of consecrating a horse and letting it loose for a year, attended by a mounted guard. The horse roamed at will, and thereby symbolized the entire control of the consecrator over the

---

[1] See Cunningham, *Num. Chron.*, 1870, p. 224. " Like all Puranic references, it is in the future, though relating to the past " (Rapson, *Coins of the Andhras*, lxiii.).

country where it wandered; any rival wishing to challenge the ruler's supremacy might do so by attempting
to seize the animal. On this particular occasion the
consecrated beast appears to have strayed as far as
the river Sindhu, and to have crossed the stream.
Menander had probably by this time begun his aggres-
sions by laying siege to Madhyamikâ (near Chitor, in
Rajputana).[1] A party of Greeks, belonging, no doubt,
to the investing army, had the temerity to take up the
challenge by attacking the horse. The defending party,
under Vasumitra, the king's grandson, managed to
beat off the "viciously valiant" barbarians, and the
hundred young Rajput nobles evidently acquitted themselves well under their youthful leader. The dramatist
represents the old king as writing enthusiastically to
his son, the warden of the marches at Bhilsa, inform-
ing him of the boy's achievement, and bidding him to
the sacrifice of the horse, which had been so manfully
preserved. Menander, however, does not appear to
have received any serious checks in his meteoric progress. Oude (Sâketa) and the ancient kingdom of
Mathura fell before the Yavana advance, and this must
have necessitated the speedy withdrawal of the Sunga
forces from the frontier town of Bhilsa, and the evacuation of the Bharut country. Menander's ambitions,
however, did not stop here. Fired by the desire to
extend his realms farther than any Greek had penetrated before, and animated, perhaps, by the ambition

---

[1] The contemporary grammarian Patanjali gives two sen-
tences, "The Yavana was besieging Saketa : the Yavana was
besieging Madhyamikâ," as examples of the Imperfect Tense,
which indicates an event which has *just* taken place.

to rival the exploits of his great prototype Asoka and restore the supremacy of Buddhism in the empire of the Mauryas, he pushed on to Pataliputra itself. Tradition says that he crossed the Sôn, but it is improbable that he actually attacked the historic capital of Middle India. Probably he only got as far as he did owing to various other troubles (notably an attack by the Raja of Kalinga upon Magadha), which distracted Pushyamitra's attention. The usual fate of an attempt at imperial policy among the Greeks overtook Menander. "The fiercely-fighting Greeks," we are told, "did not stay long in the Middle Land : a fierce strife had broken out in their own country." The miserable princelings of the Panjab, incapable of appreciating the magnificent schemes of their overlord, had, as usual, broken out into one of their suicidal faction fights. The Saka satrapies may have been giving trouble as well. It was hardly likely that a heterogeneous and scattered realm like Menander's would remain long at rest in the absence of its ruler. Menander beat a hasty retreat. The veteran Pushyamitra did not long survive his repulse of the Yavana forces,—the last European[1] invaders of India till Vasco da Gama, 1,500 years later, appeared off Calicut. Menander was one of the most powerful of the Bactrian monarchs ; indeed, there are only four of them who are of any real historical importance—Diodotus I., Euthydemus, Demetrius, and Menander. "If he really crossed the Hypanis to the east, and reached the Soanus,"[2] says

---

[1] If we can call Menander a European !

[2] *Geog.*, XI. xi., § 1. MSS. read *Isamus*. Some conjecture *Imaus;* but Menander never crossed the Himalayas. Strabo

Strabo, rather incredulously, "he must have conquered more nations than Alexander himself."

Strabo rightly reckons Menander's real achievement to have been the reconquest of the kingdom of Demetrius—the Panjab, Pattalene (Sind), and the mouth of the Indus. The author of the *Periplus*, writing, perhaps, a couple of centuries later, says that Menander's silver drachmæ were still in circulation in Broach, which shows that he fully developed the seaward commerce which his conquests had opened up. He seems to have appreciated equally the advantages of reopening the trading routes with China.[1]

Menander died some years later. Towards the end of his life he appears to have followed the example of Asoka, whom he apparently made his model, and without reliquishing the throne, to have taken the robes of the Buddhist monk.[2] It is not uncommon in Hindu and Buddhist countries for a man to devote his later years in this way to religious exercises. Death found him in the field, engaged no doubt in the interminable task of keeping order among the petty rajas of the Panjab. Tradition asserts that before death he attained the rank of an Arhat, the highest degree of sainthood of the Buddhist religion,

---

would hardly mix them up with the Paropamisus. *Iomanes* (Jumna) is a plausible conjecture. I prefer, however, *Soanus*, referring to the raid on Pataliputra. The great distance would account for Strabo's surprise. "Hypanis" is apparently the Beas (Hyphasis). For the original passage see Appendix V. (*e*), pp. 163-164.

[1] The Phrynoi and Seres of Strabo.

[2] The Chinese Emperor, Hsiao Yen, did the same. Giles, *Chinese Lit.*, p. 133.

and his ashes, like those of the Buddha, were eagerly disputed for by the states over which he had ruled. Finally, as in the former case, a compromise was effected, and, according to the common Buddhist practice, the relics were divided, and carried away to be deposited under stupas in the districts of the recipients.

Plutarch[1] has, curiously, preserved an account of his death, which is in agreement with the oriental story: "A certain Menander ruled with equity among the Bactrians and died in the field during a campaign. The states in other respects joined together in celebrating his obsequies, but over his relics a dispute arose, which was, after some difficulty, settled on the following terms: each was to take back an equal share of his ashes, that memorials[2] of the man might be set up among them all." Thus perished the "soldier-saint" of Bactria, renowned alike for his equity, his statesmanship, his military prowess, and his learning in matters secular and sacred. "In the whole of the Jambu-dipa," says the author of the *Questions*, "there was none to be compared to Milinda Raja. . . . He was endowed with riches and guarded by military power in a state of the utmost efficiency."

---

[1] In the tract *De Republica Gerenda*, p. 821. This account is, strangely enough, corroborated by a similar story found at the end of a Siamese version on the Milinda-Pañha. This is also the authority for Milinda being an Arhat at his death. Certainly his funeral was such as a reputed Arhat would enjoy. Others, however, find a parallel in the obsequies of Alexander.

[2] Μνημεῖα—*i.e.*, stupas or dâgabas (for the original text, see Appendix V.).

His coins, which are found all over Western and
North-Western India in great quantities,[1] testify to
his prosperity. His favourite emblem seems to be
the goddess Pallas,[2] who appears on eighty-four out
of ninety-five of the specimens in the Calcutta
Museum. Pallas, who also figures on the coins of
Demetrius, may have been the family emblem, as
Zeus was of the Diodoti. At any rate, she is appropriate enough to the powerful monarch, famed both
as a soldier and a scholar. She appears in various
guises: sometimes armed, or hurling the thunderbolt
at the king's enemies; while on the reverse victory
holds out a wreath for the victorious general. Many
of the coins, especially those of the elephant device,
or those bearing the figure of Hercules,[3] resemble
very closely those of Demetrius.[4] Menander appears
to have been a descendant of Demetrius, and to have
inherited his soldierly abilities and ambitions. The
king himself generally appears armed. His features
are coarse, and do not appear to be those of a man
of pure Hellenic descent. His Buddhist coins have
been already mentioned.

His death, as may be well supposed, was a signal
for a general disruption of the Bactrian kingdom. A
host of petty princes, known only by their coins,

[1] There are seventy-four in the British Museum. This is the
highest number among the Bactrian Greeks (Eucratides is next
with sixty-two), but far short of Azes, of whose coins the British
Museum has over two hundred. Ninety-five of Menander's
coins are at Calcutta.

[2] *E.g.*, Gardner, *British Museum Catalogue*, Plate XI. 8-13.

[3] Gardner, *op. cit.*, XII. 6.

[4] Gardner, III. 2.

ruled in different parts of the Panjab; and eventually
the paramount power in the north-west passed from
the Greeks to the so-called " Indo-Parthian " princes
of Taxila, who attained a considerable degree of
prosperity under their prince Maues, "Moga the
Great," as he is styled in a contemporary inscription.
Greek rule lingered faintly on for about two centuries
after Menander's death. Inscriptions in Buddhist
caves up to the second century A.D. mention gifts
by Yavana converts, who, significantly enough, bear
Indian names. Finally, the Yue-chi, the Turki tribe
which had finally become the masters of Bactria,
driving their Saka predecessors before them, began
to advance towards the Hindu-Kush. Long residence
in a settled habitation had converted these wandering
nomads into a powerful and well-organized nation.
They had adopted Buddhism, and acquired a veneer
of Indo-Greek civilization. The Bactrian Greeks
were the first to submit. Hermæus, " the last of the
Bactrians," gladly put himself under the sovereignty
of the Kushan leader, Kadphises.[1] For his lifetime he
remained a *roi fainéant*, and coins were struck at
Sâgala bearing the titles of the Scythian on the one
side and the portrait of the Greek on the other.
Lastly, the Greek ruler disappears. The latest coins
of Kadphises, bearing on the one side the Bactrian
camel, and on the other the Indian bull, mark significantly enough the final absorption of the Bactrian
Greek kings of India by their ancient enemies of
the northern steppes.[2]

[1] Kadphises I. (Kujulakarakadphises).
[2] *Circa* A.D. 50.

AUTHORITIES.

It is curious how little has been written about the great Bactrian monarch Menander. See Vincent Smith, *Early History of India*, chaps. viii., ix., and x., and *The Questions of Milinda*, translated by Dr. Rhys Davids, *Sacred Books of the East*, xxv.-xxvi. Eduard Meyer's article in the new edition of the *Encyclopædia Britannica* is a useful summary.

CHAPTER VIII

THE EFFECTS OF THE GREEK OCCUPATION ON INDIA

"The East bowed low before the blast
In patient, deep disdain;
She let the legions thunder past,
And plunged in thought again."

AND SO, less than three centuries after the Macedonian legionaries first struck terror into the Aryans of the Panjab, the last traces of Greek rule in India disappear from the page of history. No written records preserve for us the melancholy story of the gradual dwindling and final extinction of the miserable remnants of the once irresistible soldiery of Alexander; but it is not difficult to reconstruct from the numerous Græco-Indian coins handed down to us the history of their downfall. Incessant fighting was partly the cause. The "viciously valiant Yavanas," to use the contemptuous phrase of a Sanskrit writer, were for ever at war with their neighbours, when not engaged in the equally absorbing pastime of flying at one another's throats. This inherent vice of the successors to Alexander's vast empire caused its disintegration everywhere. The great conqueror's premature death had prevented him from undertaking any kind of constructive policy, and his possessions fell into the clutches of men whose trade was war, and who cared little for, and understood less of, any other. The Greeks had been forced to abandon their territories north of the Hindu-Kush because they had been " drained dry of blood " by incessant war, and the same process was repeated in India. They suffered the same fate which had overtaken Sparta some four centuries earlier.

Another equally powerful factor in obliterating Greek rule in India was the gradual process of absorption to which the coins bear such vivid witness. From Eucratides to Hermæus we perceive a steady decline of the Greek element in these records of artistic and national feeling. Greek weights and standards give place to Indian systems ; Indian inscriptions become more usual, while their Greek equivalents begin to show signs of corruption ; the figures betray, with increasing frequency, the handiwork of the native craftsman. It is tolerably easy to conjecture what was happening : the Greek, cut off from his home and all chance of intercourse with his countrymen, was intermarrying with his neighbours, with the usual effect.[1] Intermarriage between conqueror and conquered nearly always results in the absorption of the former (who are generally, as in this case, a mere handful compared with the original inhabitants), as may be seen by a glance at the remnants of Dutch and Portuguese rule in the East to-day. The very fact that Kadphises shared the throne with Hermæus seems to indicate that Scythian and Greek

---

[1] Alexander, it will be remembered, encouraged intermarriage with the natives and set the example himself. It is noteworthy that inscriptions from Buddhist caves of the first century A.D. always refer to " Yavanas " with *Hindu names* (Appendix III.).

amalgamated readily. The cosmopolitan descendants
of Alexander's colonists had, of course, none of the
Hellenic exclusiveness which formerly dubbed all non-
Greeks as "barbarians," and shunned any kind of
social intercourse with them. On the other hand,
the conservatism which distinguishes the respectable
Hindu of to-day was probably very much less in
evidence in the first century A.D. ; it dates almost entirely from the Brahminical reaction of some two
centuries after the time of which we are now speaking.
It is a curious fact that few races have disappeared so
utterly in India as the Greeks. We have, very probably, representatives of the Scythians in the Jats[1] of
the Panjab. The Parsees, who brought very few of their
females in their flight from Iran, retain their indi-
viduality completely.[2]

The Greeks, then, as a political factor, disappeared
from Indian soil before the end of the first century A.D.
We now come to a further question : Did the Greek
occupation have any effect upon the development of
Indian art or literature ? Did the contact with the
West affect, to any appreciable degree, the progress of
civilization in the East ? On this subject there has
long been a difference of opinion. Writers like Weber
and Niese, carried away by the enthusiasm of their
discoveries of similarities, often purely fortuitous,
between the art and literature of India and Greece, have

[1] Jat is the same word as "Getæ," in all probability. Others,
less plausibly, identify them with the Zanthii of Strabo, or the
Iatii of Pliny. Cunningham, *Arch. Survey Reports*, II., 54 *ff*.

[2] For foreign elements in India and the process by which
they were absorbed, see Mr. Bhandarkar's able paper in the
Indian Antiquary, January, 1911.

formed a very exaggerated opinion of the influence of Greek culture upon the East. It is easy, of course, to find parallels, more or less close, between the legends and speculations of both countries. The story of the rape of Helen in the Iliad bears a general resemblance to the central theme of the *Ramayana;* the Orphic doctrines of metempsychosis and retributive justice are very similar to the theories which have formed the basis of Hindu religious speculation since the time of the Upanishads. There is no solid ground, however, for supposing that during the Bactrian period either Hindu or Greek knew much of the language or literature of the other. The Greeks were notoriously scornful of the achievements of the " barbarians,"[1] and for an outsider to learn Sanskrit in those days would have been a sheer impossibility, owing to Brahminical opposition to and the lack of written works in that language.

How superficial was the real knowledge about India, even of a Greek who had been long resident in the country, may be gathered from such remarks as that of Megasthenes that the Indians worshipped Hercules and Dionysus.[2] The Hindus were equally indifferent to Greek influence, which was essentially repugnant to the exclusive Brahminical tradition, and only made itself felt among the cosmopolitan dwellers in the Pan-

---

[1] Ctesias is another notorious instance. Though resident for years at the Persian Court, he was unable, or unwilling, to learn enough of the Avesta tongue to read the invaluable documents which must have then been accessible. In consequence his history is a valueless mass of legends.

[2] Hercules was the mace-bearing Shiva. The legend connecting Dionysus with India was most persistent.

jab. Considerably later, probably in the second and third centuries after Christ, we find Hindu writers betraying a certain acquaintance with Greek astronomy; but it is doubtful whether this implies a knowledge of Greek by Indian philosophers, as no other branches of Indian learning (Logic for instance), show any signs of western influence.[1] Professor Weber quotes in support of his contention a statement of St. Chrysostom (A.D. 117). St. Chrysostom writes as follows: "It is said that the poetry of Homer is sung by the Indians, who had translated it into their own language and modes of expression. . . . They are not unacquainted with the woes of Priam, and the weeping and wailing of Andromache and Hecuba, and the heroic feats of Achilles and Hector, so potent was the influence of what man had sung."[2] This assertion, however, need not be taken very seriously; it is probably based upon travellers' stories of the general resemblances of the Hindu epics to Greek tales. Similar statements, of no greater value, are found in Plutarch and Ælian.[3] Plutarch says that through Alexander Asia was civilized and Homer became known there; Ælian asserts that the Indians and Persians have translated the poems of Homer, "if we may believe those who have written on these subjects."

The extravagant theories of Weber, Windisch, Niese, and others, led to a natural reaction. Later writers, among whom Mr. Vincent Smith is perhaps the most

---

[1] Apparently the Hindus knew something about Greek medicine at an earlier date.

[2] *Or.*, LIII., § 554. McCrindle, *Ancient India*, p. 177.

[3] *Ver. Hist.*, XII., 48.

prominent, have been disposed to deny that the
Bactrian Greeks exerted any appreciable influence
upon India whatever. They contend that the occupation of India by the Greeks who followed Eucratides
and Menander was purely a military and commercial
matter; and the invaders were swept away, just as
the relics of Alexander's invasion had been swept
away, without leaving any permanent traces behind
them.

Writers who hold this view argue that it is not likely
that rough and illiterate Macedonian soldiers and their
(probably in many instances half-caste) descendants
would have any great knowledge of Greek literature,
much less imbue their neighbours with a taste for it. They
point out, moreover, that not a single Greek inscription
belonging to the Bactrian period has been unearthed in
India, and they come to the conclusion that palpable
evidences of an active Hellenism have not been found
in the East. "The history of these Greek dynasties,"
says the writer of an important article on this subject
in the new *Encyclopædia*, "is for us almost a blank, and
for estimating the amount and quality of Hellenism in
Bactria, we are reduced to building hypotheses upon
the scantiest data." This is undeniably true; the
thick mists of obscurity, which unhappily hang like a
pall upon the early history of India, make anything
approaching to certainty impossible. But this very
fact makes it almost as rash to deny Greek influence
in toto as to make too much of it; and one or two
considerations make it appear highly probable that
the Greek settlers in India were not altogether the
" illiterate military colonists " that the anti-Hellenists

would have us suppose them to have been. First and foremost, the splendid coins which distinguish the Bactrian empire can only have been the work of an extremely cultivated race. Mr. W. W. Tarn,[1] one of the opponents of the Hellenic theory, is driven to the somewhat desperate expedient of declaring them to be a " sport," the result of a spasmodic outburst of genius. That they were, on the contrary, the product of a highly artistic nation is far more probable. The traditions of Menander and his capital at Sâgala, as preserved in the *Milinda Panha*, appear to indicate that the Bactrian Greeks were a cultured nation at the time of their greatest prosperity. The description of the Greek monarch's court seems to show that he was not a mere semi-barbarous conqueror, but a ruler who, if he did not seek to rival the great cities of the Ptolemies or the Seleucids, at any rate upheld the traditions of Hellenic civilization in a not unworthy manner. The fact that long after the extinction of Greek rule their Scythian successors continued to use Greek or semi-Greek inscriptions on their coins seems to show that the language had considerable prestige in Sâgala, and perhaps other towns of Western India ; it may even have been the court language of the Indo-Scythian and Indo-Parthian rulers. The paucity of Greek inscriptions of the period does, indeed, lend some colour to Mr. Tarn's assertions ; but even here, though we must not make too much of the fact, we should remember that archæology in India is still in its infancy—the Kabul Valley is practically untouched—and even the last

[1] *J.H.S.*, vol. xxii., p. 268.

twelve months have brought to light many valuable discoveries, modifying considerably our views upon Græco-Indian art. The famous Gandhara sculptures belong, of course, not to the period of the Greek occupation, but to the more settled and prosperous rule of the powerful Scythian monarchs who succeeded them. But were these works of art the product of indigenous workmen, descendants of the Bactrian Greeks whose artistic powers found such magnificent expression in their coins, or were they the work of outsiders, called in from distant countries for the purpose?' Perhaps Bactrian Greeks were employed more generally than is usually supposed in connection with these undertakings.[1] It does not appear to be likely that imported artists were employed in the great numbers that would have been required to execute the numberless friezes, statues, and bas-reliefs which have been discovered. On the other hand, an inscription discovered by Mr. Marshall near Bhilsa in 1909[2] shows very clearly that during the rule of the Bactrian kings Bactro-Greek workmen were employed in India, being lent, no doubt, on account of their technical proficiency, to Indian rajas. This inscription, which is of the utmost importance in the study of the question of Greek influence on Indian art, was found on a pillar surmounted by an image of Garud. It runs as follows:[3] "On behalf of Kasiputra Bhagabhadra, the Saviour, King of Samkasya, King Chandradasa caused this Garud pillar of Vasudeva, God of Gods, to be made by the

---

[1] See Appendix III.
[2] *J.R.A.S.*, 1909, p. 1053 *ff.*; *vide* Appendix III.
[3] *Ibid.*, p. 1092.

Greek, Heliodorus, son of Dion, of Taxila, a worshipper
of Bhagavat, who had been sent by the Maharaja
Antialkidas."

Here, then, we have very strong evidence of the
existence of Bactro-Greek sculptors. Heliodorus is
no outsider called in from the West. He is a subject
of Antialkidas,[1] and, what is still more remarkable, a
convert to Hinduism, which points unmistakably to
his eastern origin. Further proof is found in the
likeness between much of the Gandhara work and the
coins of the later Bactrian kings. A Triton group
with serpent legs (evidently a reminiscence of the
Pergamene sculptures), in the Lahore Museum, resembles very remarkably a similar design on coins
of Hippostratus.[2] Marine subjects, Tritons fighting
with gods, and so forth, are commonly used for
decorative purposes, just as Poseidon and other
maritime subjects appear on Bactrian coins. Antimachus, it will be remembered, struck coins bearing
the figure of Poseidon. It is curious to find sculptures
of this character in kingdoms so many hundreds of
miles from the coast. It has been suggested that the
Greeks never got over their first surprise at the sight
of the mighty Indus, which appeared to them more
like an inland sea than a river. A peculiarly
beautiful example of Græco-Indian workmanship was
the priceless reliquary discovered by Dr. Spooner in
the remains of the great Stûpa of Kaniska, near
Peshawar, in 1909. This, again, was the work of
a Greek artist, for it bears an inscription to the

[1] 170 B.C.
[2] See, *e.g.*, Gardner, Plate XIV. 6.

effect that it was made by "Agesilaos, overseer at Kaniska Vihâra."[1]

Kaniska was a fervent supporter of Buddhism. During his reign shrines sprang up in every direction in North-Western India, and the adaptable Greek workman of the East was as ready to use his technical skill for the portrayal of Buddhist scenes, as his western kinsmen were to accommodate themselves to the foreign deities, Mithra, Isis, and the rest, who about the same time began to find a place in the Roman Pantheon.[2] Moreover, the Indo-Greek culture which thus became associated with Buddhism spread far beyond the borders of Hindustan. Recent explorations have unearthed, in what are at present vast sandy steppes in distant Khotan, remains of once populous cities, where fragments of Buddhist manuscripts in the Kharoshthi character are mingled with seals, carvings, and bas-reliefs of an unmistakably Greek type.[3]

It is difficult to estimate, with the evidence we have, the precise nature of the debt of Indian art to Greece. It is true that we have no artistic remains in India which belong to the pre-Alexandrian period. The truth is, before the time of Asoka (272-

[1] *J.R.A.S.*, 1909, p. 1058.

[2] "Les sculpteurs qui pour le bénéfice des pieux donateurs du Gandhara adaptèrent le type d'Apollon à la représentation des divinités bouddhiques, semblent bien les petits-cousins de ceux qui vers le même époque coiffaient le Mithra persan au bonnet phrygien de Ganymède . . . et donnaient au Jésus des Catacombs les traits d'Orphée ou du bon Pasteur" (Foucher, *L'Art du Gandhara*, I.

[3] Aurel Stein, *Sand-buried Cities of Khotan*, p. 396, etc.

231 B.C.) stone was very little used for sculpture; in the Bhilsa carvings and other early Buddhist work we can still plainly trace the influence of wood-carving in the treatment of the stone.[1] The "Buddhist rail" pattern, for instance, is an imitation in stone of an actual wooden railing, used in earlier times for fencing in the *stupa*. On the other hand, it would be impossible to say that the Greeks taught India the art of carving in stone, as the earliest stone monuments, the Bhilsa carvings and the Asoka pillar at Sarnath, show no signs whatever of Greek influence; the latter is obviously Persian rather than Greek. The same applies to Indian architecture; the earliest structures, like the Karla caves, show no traces of Greek influence.[2] The Indo-Greek school of the Kushan period, with its Corinthian and Ionic pillars and stucco ornaments, is a purely local and exotic product. The practice of using regular coins, properly stamped and shaped, in the place of rude punch-marked ingots, may have been introduced by the Greeks; the Indians, however, never excelled in the art of coining, and their best coins were only clumsy imitations of Greek models. While, then, we may safely deny that the Bactrian Greeks, or other "Yavana" settlers, exercised any appreciable influence on Indian art, it is important to realize that the contact with the West imparted an immense

---

[1] Wooden groins of great antiquity still span the roof of the *Chaitya* at Karle.

[2] And yet, curiously enough, they were largely due to the pious gifts, if not the actual work, of "Yavanas," *vide* Appendix III. In the same way the Garud pillar, already referred to, is quite Indian in style.

impetus to India; it was like an electric shock, waking the land to new life, after the lethargy of countless years of undisturbed peace. The vigorous rule of the Maurya monarchs, which saw the beginnings of a great Indian renaissance, was indirectly the result of Alexander's invasion. But the Gandhara, or Indo-Greek school of architecture and sculpture, is almost entirely foreign, and influenced India very little. It was the work of foreign artists, patronized by foreign kings, and was completely swept away in the Brahminical revival of the fourth century A.D. The Gandhara sculptures are not very high art, from either the Greek or the Indian point of view, though they are of immense interest to the student of Buddhism, recording, as they do, the legends and episodes of the life of Gautama in a unique manner.[1]

Turning from art to literature, we are confronted with the question whether the post-Grecian literature of India was influenced by the contact with the Bactrian invaders. It has been already shown how futile have been the efforts to detect any traces of such influence in earlier times; but it is often claimed that the Indian drama, at least, shows much clearer signs of western contact. It is perfectly possible that Greek plays were acted at Sâgala, and perhaps other Indo-Greek cities,[2] and may even have been occasion-

---

[1] Did the practice of *idolatry* come to India from Greece? No sculptures of Buddha, or of any Hindu gods, are found in the early Hindu or Buddhist remains.

[2] Plutarch (*Vit. Alex.*) states that, after Alexander's invasion, "the children of Persians, Gedrosians, and Susians, sang the tragedies of Euripides and Sophocles."

ally performed in the presence of the Kushan kings, who affected Greek culture. Any *a priori* arguments as to the improbabilty of the Bactrian Greeks having "any time or energy left for such things as art, science, and culture,"[1] apply equally well to the anti-Hellenic and semi-civilized Parthians; yet everyone knows the story of the company which was acting the "Bacchæ" before the court when the news of the Battle of Carrhæ arrived. Unfortunately, the evidence for any direct influence is extremely slight. Dramas were known in India, as we learn from the *Mahâbhâshya* of Patanjali, at the time when Bactro-Greek rule was flourishing; but the only plays which have come down to us belong to a much later period. The introduction of the *Yavanikâ*, or "Greek Curtain,"[2] is probably due to later Græco-Roman influence, as it is improbable that a curtain was used at all on the Greek stage. Similarly, the frequent appearance of "Yavani slaves" on the stage as the attendants of princes represents an everyday feature of Indian court-life. Greek girls (from Syria and Egypt) were

---

[1] W. W. Tarn, *J.H.S.*, 1902, p. 292.

[2] The term *Yavanikâ* probably means a curtain made of Greek fabric. The curtain *may* have been suggested by someone who had seen Roman plays. Yavanîs are usually armour-bearers; the term, like the French *Suisses*, is quite vague. These terms do not indicate Greek influence, but merely that the Yavanas were in India at the time of the rise of the drama. The drama certainly flourished at the time of Patanjali, the contemporary of Menander; it *may* be as old as Panini (350 B.C.). Fragments of a Buddhist drama, by Asvaghosa, Kaniskha's court-poet, have been unearthed in Central Asia (Rapson, Art. *Indian Drama*, in Hastings' *Dictionary of Religion and Ethics*).

often sent to India as presents, or by way of tribute.
Weber's attempt to trace in the *Mricchakatika* the
influence of Menander, is about on a par with his
endeavour to connect the *Ramayana* and the Iliad.
As a matter of fact, the florid classical drama of
India is no more like the severe austerity of the
Greek stage than a Dravidian shrine is like a Greek
temple. Their only point of similarity is the avoid-
ance by both of violent action on the stage. Indian
dramas, with their prologues, their mixture of comic
and pathetic (the " clown " is a regular feature in
Indian plays), and their disregard of the " unities,"
are really far more like the Elizabethan dramas of
England. This, as Professor Macdonell remarks, is
an instructive instance of how similar developments
can arise independently. It should serve as a warning to those who seize upon every chance coincidence
to try and detect traces of Hellenic " influence " in
India.

We are not now concerned with the effects of the
close intercourse between India and the later Roman
empire. Its extent is indicated by the frequent
references to India by Greek and Roman writers, and
by the great numbers of Roman coins found in different parts of the country. An unmistakably
Oriental cast of thought may be distinguished in
Neo-Platonism, and in many phases of early Chris-
tianity. Alexandria, the emporium of eastern trade,
was especially a point of contact. The anchorites of
the Egyptian deserts were not very far from the
Hylobioi and *Sramanaioi*, the Brahman and Buddhist
ascetics, mentioned by Clement of Alexandria. On

the other hand, Indian astronomy betrays the fact that the borrowing was not all on one side. Two out of five of the Indian *Siddhantas*, or systems, come from the West. The *Romaka Siddhanta* is obviously western ; the *Paulisa Siddhanta* is probably based on the works of Paul of Alexandria (*circa* A.D. 378). At least one Greek astronomical term has passed into the classical language of India.[1]

Did the Greek invasion exercise any political influence upon India ? This is not the least interesting of the questions falling within the scope of the present discussion. It seems more than probable that Alexander taught India what he had already demonstrated to the West, and that is, the idea of a great world-wide monarchy replacing the petty city-states which appear to have been almost universal in primitive Aryan communities. It may be argued, of course, that Chandragupta, the founder of the Maurya dynasty, and the first to try and realize the great ideal of the *Chakkavatti Raja*, the "Universal King," did not need the example of Alexander. He might have obtained his ideas from the older Achæmenian monarchy, and the use of Persian terms, such as *chhatrapa* (*satrap*) on Indian coins, may point in this direction.[2]

---

[1] व्यामिच, obviously the Greek διάμετρον. It is used by Kalidas (*Kumarasambhava*, Canto VII.) in the sense of a sign of the zodiac—the seventh place on the horoscope, says Mallinath. Indian astronomy is full of Greek terms—*e.g.*, Âra (Ἄρης), *Heli* (Ἥλιος), *Jyan* (Ζεύς), *kriya* (κρίος), *tâvuri* (ταῦρος), *pâthona* (παρθένος), *jituma* (δίδυμος), *âkokera* (αἰγοκέρως) *trikona* (τρίγωνος), etc. See Von Schroeder, *Indiens Literatur and Cultur*, p. 726.

[2] But this word was borrowed from the Parthians, who were in close touch with Bactria, and not direct from Persia. The

On the other hand, the Maurya monarchs, who re-volutionized the Indian system of government, had no dealings with the Persian empire, which had been over-thrown before their advent; with the Hellenic world, on the contrary, the Mauryas were always in the closest touch. Some of the semi-Hellenic monarchs of the Middle East in the post-Alexandrian period, were in the habit of assuming the title of "Philhellen" to show their sympathies with Greek culture. This title might have been appropriately borne by Chandragupta and his successors. Chandragupta himself used to recall with pride, it is said, his meeting with the great con-queror in his youth, and a significant story tells of how he worshipped at the gigantic altars which the Mace-donians had erected on the banks of the Hyphasis before they turned back. Chandragupta married a Greek princess, and the Greek writer Megasthenes was a resident at his court, as Deimachus was at the court of his successor Bindusara. Stories have been preserved indicating the intimacy between the Indian and Syrian courts, and exchanges of presents and gifts of wine and drugs are mentioned. It is even possible that Greek teachers were sent to instruct these enlightened monarchs in the wisdom of the West.[1] All things considered, it is difficult to escape the con-

---

word *Chakravarti* is, of course, as old as the time of Gautama Buddha. Older monarchs had partially succeeded in subduing their neighbours—*e.g.*, Ajatâsatru, but to nothing like the same extent as Chandragupta.

[1] The influence of the West was strongest under Chandragupta, and died out after Asoka. Of course the *court* of Chandragupta was no more western than that of an enlightened eastern prince of to-day is.

clusion that Greek ideas must have penetrated more freely than is usually supposed into India in the Maurya dynasty, and it seems almost impossible to deny the extreme probability that these rulers owed to Alexander their imperial conceptions. The great conqueror's name is still remembered all over the East, and the magic of his personality can hardly have failed to excite the admiration and emulation of his Indian contemporaries and successors.[1]

AUTHORITIES.

These are summarized exhaustively by Professor Macdonell, *History of Sanskrit Literature* (Bibliographical Notes to chap. xvi.). Mr. V. A. Smith (*Early History of India*) is one of the chief opponents of the theory of Greek influence in India. See also the highly important article by W. W. Tarn, in the *Journal of Hellenic Studies*, vol. xxii. : "Notes on Hellenism in Bactria and India." For the Gandhara sculptures, M. Foucher is the leading authority (*L'Art du Gandhara, Sur La Frontière Indo-Afghane*, etc.). See also Sir W. W. Hunter, *Imperial Gazetteer of India*, 1881, vol. iv., p. 261. A highly important article on "Hellenism" appears in the eleventh edition of the *Encyclopædia Britannica*.

---

[1] It should be added, however, that Alexander's name is unknown in Hindu literature. It was brought to India by the Mahommedans. Alexander subdued Persia. He only touched the fringe of India

APPENDICES

APPENDIX I

RULERS OF BACTRIA

I. Prehistoric Dynasties of Eastern Iran.

II. Persian Empire.

Persian Kings.	Satraps of Bactria.
Cyrus, 550—529 B.C.	Smerdis, son of Cyrus, executed by Cambyses.
Cambyses, 529—522 B.C.	? Hystaspes (Vistaspa), father of Darius, satrap of Eastern Iran.
Darius I., 521—485 B.C.	Dardases.
Xerxes I., 485—464 B.C.	i. Masistes (murdered).
	ii. Hystaspes (revolts on accession of Artaxerxes).
Artaxerxes I., 464—424 B.C.	
Xerxes II., 424—423 B.C.	? Secydianus or Sogdianus, brother of the king, who eventually murders him.
Darius II., 423—404 B.C.	?

Persian Kings.	*Satraps of Bactria.*
Artaxerxes II., 404—358 B.C.	?
Artaxerxes III., 358—336 B.C.	?
Oarses, ? 336—335 B.C.	?
Darius III., 335—330 B.C.	Bessus, cousin of Darius (?).
	Oxyartes (Sogdia) cousin of Darius (?).

(Bessus assumes the title of Artaxerxes IV., and is acknowledged by the princes of Eastern Iran; captured 329—328 B.C.)

III. BACTRIA UNDER ALEXANDER AND HIS SUCCESSORS.

	Governors of Bactria.
Alexander, 328—323 B.C.	Artabazus. (Clitus.) Amyntas. Tyriaspes, ⎱ Governors of Oxyartes, ⎰ Paropamisus.
Partition of Triparadisus, 321 B.C.	Stasanor of Soli. ? Philip. ? Nicanor.
Seleucus I., 312—281 B.C.	
Antiochus I., 280—261 B.C.	?
Antiochus II., 261—246 B.C.	Theodotus (revolted 250 B.C.).

IV. BACTRIA AS AN INDEPENDENT KINGDOM.

(a) *Kings of Bactria Proper.*

Diodotus I., 250—245 B.C.[1]
Diodotus II., 245—230 B.C.
(Antimachus Theos, a pretender.)
Euthydemus of Magnesia, 230—200 B.C.

(b) *Kings of Bactria and Sâgala.*

Demetrius, 200—160 B.C.
Eucratides, 160—156 B.C.
Apollodotus, 156 B.C. (?)
Heliocles, 156—136 B.C. (Evacuation of Bactria about 135 B.C.)

(c) *Kings of Sâgala.*

Heliocles, 135 B.C.—?.
Menander, Emperor of the whole of the Panjab and Kabul, *circa* 165—130 B.C.

(d) *Subordinate Monarchs*[2] (petty rulers subordinate to Bactria or Sâgala, owning small principalities in Kabul or Panjab) 160 B.C.—A.D. 45.

KABUL.

Euthydemus II.	Amyntas.
Archebius.	Hermæus, *last Greek ruler*
Antimachus II.	*in India, circa* A.D. 45.

[1] The dates here given are mostly purely conjectural; authorities differ widely on the subject.

[2] It is really futile in our present state of knowledge to try and arrange, still less to date, these petty princes, only known by their coins. See Vincent Smith, *Early History of India*, Appendices to chap. ix.

PANJAB.

Pantaleon.	Dionysius.	Artemidorus.
Agathocles.	Apollophanes.	Epander.
Agathocleia.	Lysias.	Nicias.
Strato I.	Theophilus.	Telephus.
Strato II.	Hippostratus.	Antialcidas.
Plato (165 B.C.).	Peucelaus.	Philoxenus.
Zoilus.	Diomedes.	

APPENDIX II

SOME PROBLEMS RAISED BY THE COINAGE OF EUCRATIDES

1. A COIN figured by Gardner (*Catalogue*, etc., p. 19) has caused a good deal of trouble to numismatists. Gardner and the older authorities read the inscription on it as KARISIYE NAGARA DEVATA, " God of the city of Karisi." The identity of the mysterious "City of Karisi" caused much expenditure of ingenuity. Von Gutschmid identified it with "Charis in Aria" (*Encyclopædia Britannica*, vol. xviii., p. 591, footnote, column 1). Rhys Davids, in his introduction to the *Questions of Milinda*, showed that it was "philologically possible " to connect it with Kalasi on the Indus, the birthplace of Milinda-Menander! Professor Rapson,[1] however, has shown that the reading on the coin is not KARISIYE, but KAVISIYE. This simplifies the problem immensely. "KAVISI" is *KAPISA*, the name given to North-Eastern Afghanistan, the country north of the

---

[1] Rapson, *J.R.A.S.*, 1905, p. 784. The suggestion was first made by Marquardt. These coins were also issued by Apollodotus and restruck by Eucratides. This complicates matters : who was Apollodotus ? If he was the predecessor of Eucratides, he cannot have been his murderer. Yet he seems to have been a contemporary of Menander. *Cf.* pp. 85, 112 *n.*

Kabul River. It is roughly equivalent to the Ki-pin of the Chinese annalists, though Ki-pin seems to include part of Kashmir as well (V. A. Smith, p. 220 note). The coin in this case was merely struck to celebrate some conquest of Eucratides over the country to the south of the Parapamisus ; perhaps it was issued when he had won his great victory over Demetrius for local circulation, to emphasize the change of rulers.

2. A more difficult problem is raised by the series (Gardner, Plate VII., 9-10) bearing the inscriptions : ΕΥΚΡΑΤΙΔΗΣ · ΗΛΙΟΚΛΕΟΥΣ · ΚΑΙ · ΛΑΟΔΙΚΗΣ.

It seems fairly clear that Laodice is a Seleucid princess, and the most reasonable supposition is that she was the daughter of Demetrius by his marriage with the daughter of Antiochus III. This seems fairly probable ; and, supposing for the moment we take it for granted, we are confronted by the problem, *Who is the Heliocles of the coins ?*

Perhaps it would be better to classify the views which have been, or may be, held on the subject :

(a) Heliocles is the son of Eucratides,[1] who afterwards succeeded him. It is possible that after deposing Demetrius, Eucratides attempted to conciliate his rivals by marrying his daughter to a prince of the fallen house, and this policy, too, might prevent any trouble with the Seleucid kings. It is noticeable

---

[1] Professor Ed. Meyer, in the new *Encyclopædia Britannica*, says that Heliocles is "probably his son," and the coins celebrate his marriage to Laodice, " who may have been a Seleucid princess."

that Laodice,[1] a princess in her own right, is *crowned* on the coins with the royal fillet; Heliocles, being merely a prince, has no insignia.[2] This seems to fit in with the views of von Sallet and von Gutschmid and others.

(b) Gardner, however, has a strong argument to urge against this view. Can we possibly interpret the inscription in any other way but by supposing the ellipse of the usual ΤΙΟΣ? The view stated above compels us to supply ΠΑΤΗΡ, which would be most unnatural. It seems as if the inscription *must* bear its natural interpretation, "Eucratides, *son of* Heliocles and Laodice," and this view is supported strongly by the fact that the people figured in the coins are both *elderly*, and by the fact that Heliocles is not crowned—he lived and died a private citizen, though husband of a princess. The theory is further confirmed when we remember that in Greece it was extremely common to name a child after its grandfather. We are pretty certain that Eucratides had a *son* named Heliocles, and that lends additional probability to the supposition that his *father* was named Heliocles too. If we take it as proved that the persons represented on the coins are the parents of Eucratides —and the cumulative evidence seems to point most curiously in favour of that conclusion—we are left to choose between two views, which we will label (c) and (d) respectively.

(c) *Eucratides was the grandson of his rival and predecessor Demetrius through Laodicé, the latter's daughter.* This is a bold view, but may be the

---

[1] *Vide Catalogue*, Plate V., 6-9.　[2] *Ibid.*, Plate VI., 6, 7.

true one. Demetrius was married soon after the siege of Bactria, and Laodicé, if she is his daughter, might have been born as early as 206 B.C. But in that case Eucratides, at the earliest, could hardly have been born before 192 B.C. We have strong grounds for believing that his accession to the throne took place in 174 B.C., as that was the date of the accession of Mithradates; and Justin expressly tells us (XLI. 6, 1) that they both came to the throne about the same time. But according to this theory, he was only eighteen when he achieved his final victory, and that after a long conflict. This would certainly be a remarkable achievement for a mere boy. Again, if this be the case, we must put back the date of the death of Eucratides, as he certainly could not have had a son old enough to murder him and declare himself king (as described by Justin, XLI. 6) in 165 B.C., at which date Eucratides was himself under thirty on this hypothesis. But the date may be wrong.

(d) Perhaps the most tenable theory is, that the Heliocles of the coins *is* the father of Eucratides, and Laodice his mother; but that the latter was *not* the *daughter* of Demetrius by his Seleucid wife, but a relation—sister, cousin, or some such connection—who had accompanied her to Bactria, perhaps, when she was married to the young prince. On the other hand, Laodice is certainly a name which would point to *direct* descent from a Seleucid king (the first Laodice was the mother of the founder of the dynasty); and a striking point in favour of this theory (c) is found in the medals of Agathocles, described on p. 98. Agathocles apparently issues these medals in commemoration of his royal ancestors, and amongst these (they include Alexander the Great and Diodotus) is one which bears the image and superscription of "Antiochus Nicator." I have tried to prove, on pp. 98-99, that this is Antiochus III.; and if so, it seems that Agathocles traces his descent through a long line of kings back to Antiochus— *i.e.*, that children of Demetrius and his Seleucid wife actually occupied the throne.

APPENDIX III

GREEK WORKMEN IN INDIA

OF late years it has been the fashion to minimize the influence of Greek Art on India. Messrs. Havell and Coomaraswamy have vindicated the independence of the Indian artistic tradition; and it has been shown that the Gandhara sculptures belonged to the Indo-Scythian, and not to the Bactrian dynasties. Mr. V. A. Smith looks upon the Greek occupation of the Panjab as purely military. An important inscription, however, has just been discovered which records that Greek workmen *did* work in India in the times of the Bactrian kings, and may, therefore, have influenced native craftsmen very considerably. The inscription is unique because it is the only contemporary Indian record of the Bactrian kings:

"For the sake of Kâshîputra-Bhâgabhadra, the Saviour, king of Sâmkâsya; King Chandadâsa caused the Garud pillar of Vâsudeva, God of Gods, to be made here by Heliodorus son of Dion, a votary of Bhagavat, a *Yona-data*[1] (Greek) of Takhasila, who came from the Maharaja Antalkidas." The inscription is in Kharoshthi. It was found by Dr. Marshall at

---

[1] ? *Dûta*—*i.e.*, an emissary from the Greeks.

Besnagar, in Mâlwâ. (The translation is Dr. Fleet's. For the original see *J.R.A.S.*, 1909, p. 1092.)

Another interesting inscription was that on the Buddha casket found in Kanishka's *stupa* at Peshawar, (*J.R.A.S.*, 1909, p. 1058), recording that it was made by "Agesilaos, overseer of works at Kanishka's vihara, in the Sangarâma of Mahasêna." (*Dasa agisala navakarmi kaniskasa viharê Mahasênasa Sangarâmê.*) Though this was actually after the extinction of Greek rule, there were evidently many Greek craftsmen employed in the raja's courts. The *stupa* has Corinthian pillars.[1]

It is interesting to notice in the various Buddhist caves in the Bombay Presidency that the names of Yavana donors of sculptures, cisterns, pillars, etc., frequently occur.[2] In the case of the Karla caves, some of these inscriptions date from the second century A.D., and point to the continuance of Græco-Buddhist settlements at quite a late date. Inscriptions Nos. 7 and 10 (*Bombay Gazeteer*, vol. xviii.), refer to pillars, the gifts of Sihadhaya and Dhama, Yavanas from Dhenukâkata.[3] Perhaps these Yavanas took

---

[1] It should be noticed that while the Peshawar casket is Greek or Indo-Greek in type, the Garud pillar from Bhilsa, like the so-called Yavana work in the Buddhist caves, is purely Indian. The reading Agisala has been questioned.

[2] The earliest mention of Yavana workmanship appears to be in the Girnar inscription in Kathiawar, which records that the Girnar Lake was "furnished with conduits by the Yavana Raja Tushaspa for Asoka." Tushaspa appears by his name to have been a Persian, a relic of the Alexandrian conquest.

[3] Benâkatakâ in the Nasik district. See Rapson, *Andhra Cat.*, Introd., xxix., xlvii.

Buddhist names on their conversion.[1] So the Yavanas in the Milinda-Panha have (apparently) Indian names. Or perhaps they retained very little of their Greek origin except a tradition of their birth.

In the Nâsik caves we find one *lena* owned by "Indrâgnidatta, son of Dhammadeva, a Yonaka from the north, from Dattamitra." Here both father and son appear to have Hindu names. Their residence, Dattamitra, in Sind, is thought to have been founded by Demetrius.

In the Junnar caves we have three inscriptions referring to Greeks : one of them is named "Irila,"[2] which sounds suspiciously like a Greek name, perhaps Euryalus, or something of that kind.

(See the *Indian Antiquary*, January, 1911, pp. 12-14 etc.)

---

[1] So the Chinese pilgrims took the title of Sakyaputra (Shih in Chinese).

[2] *Arch. Sur. W. India*, iv., No. 5, p. 92.

APPENDIX IV

THE SPREAD OF BUDDHISM IN THE NORTH-WEST OF INDIA

THERE is no proof positive that Buddhism became the religion of the Bactrian kings of Sâgala. There is, however, nothing against such a supposition; the probabilities, indeed, are in its favour. That converts were made, even to the more conservative Hinduism, among the Greeks has been proved by the inscription quoted in Appendix III. Asoka was anxious to make Greek converts, and in later days there were colonies of "Yavana" Buddhists, as the Karla Cave inscriptions show. Agathocles is the first prince to mint coins with Buddhist symbols. Menander, curiously enough, besides the epithet *dhramikâsa* (Δικαίου), has nothing very definitely Buddhist in his coinage; but the evidence for his conversion seems, to my mind, overwhelming. Firstly, there is the tradition embodied in the *Milinda Pañha*, which, I think, is certainly *not* a mere romance of the type of Xenophon's *Cryopædia*. Secondly there is the story of his funeral. In Plutarch's tract *Reipublicæ Gerendæ Præcepta*, p. 821, occurs the following passage:

"A certain Menander ruled with equity among the Bactrians, and died in the field during a campaign. The states in other respects joined together in celebrating his obsequies, but over his relics a dispute arose among them, which was after some difficulty settled upon the following terms : each was to take back an equal share of his ashes, that memorials (μνήμεια = stupas, dâgabas) might be set up among them all." [1] Now, this is precisely the kind of funeral which was accorded to Gautama Buddha, as described in the *Maha-Parinibbana-sutta* (S.B.E. XI., p. 131). There, too, seven tribes met and quarrelled over his ashes, and were finally pacified by an agreement that each should take a part. These were taken by the recipients to their own countries and enshrined in dâgabas.

This practice is practically peculiar to Buddhism, and confirms the Siamese tradition of Menander's conversion, and even of his attainment of Arhatship. [2]

It make be taken for granted that Buddhism made converts pretty freely among the various foreign tribes on the North-Western Frontier. [3] It finally became the religion of the Kushans, and under Kaniska reached its climax. This popularity of

---

[1] Μενάνδρου δὲ τινός ἐν Βάκτροις ἐπιεικῶς βασιλεύσαντος εἶτ' ἀποθανόντος ἐπὶ στρατοπέδον, τὴν μὲν ἄλλην ἐποιήσαντο κηδειάν κατὰ τὸ κοινὸν αἱ πόλεις· περὶ δὲ τῶν λειψάνων αὐτοῦ καταστάντες εἰς ἀγῶνα, μόλις συνέβησαν, ὥστε νειμάμενοι μέρος ἴσον τῆς τέφρας ἀπελθεῖν καὶ γενέσθαι μνημεῖα παρα πᾶσι τοῦ ἀνδρός.

[2] Von Gutschmid, however, compares what happened on the death of Alexander.

[3] *E.g.*, the Greeks, the Indo-Parthians (so-called), and the Yue-Chi.

Buddhism among the Scythian tribes from Peshawar to Balkh and Khotan, raises the interesting question whether Gautama himself did not belong to a clan which was Scythian by origin. If the Sakyas *were* originally Sakas (Sacæ or Scythians), it would account for many of the puzzling features of that creed: its unmetaphysical and un-Indian character, (in spite of the Indian garb in which it was, naturally enough, put forward), its attack on caste, abhorrence of bloodshed, worship of relics, etc. The *dâgaba*, or *stûpa*, which is such a feature of Buddhism, has been traced to the conical Tartar tents by Fergusson and others.[1] The " ancestral temples " of the Scythians described by Herodotus (IV. 62, 72, 124, etc.) may have been rude dâgabas erected to cover the body of the semi-divine chieftain and the victims who accompanied him. One of the keenest of the clans who strove for relics of the Buddha were the *Vaggi of Vesali*. Beal (*Life of Hiuen Tsang*, §§ 5-7, *J.R.A.S.*, XIV. 39, etc.) has tried to show that these are none other than the Yue-Chi, and as such appear in regular Scythic garb on the Sanchi sculptures. If this is so, there were Scythians in India in the days of Gautama, and there is no reason to doubt that the Sakyas, like the Vaggi, were two clans of this nation.

[1] Or to the shape of the funeral pyre.

APPENDIX V

PASSAGES IN ANCIENT AUTHORS REFERRING TO BACTRIA

I. Justin.

(a) Opulentissimum illud mille urbium Bactrianum imperium.—XLI. 1.

(b) Hi (Parthi) postea, diductis Macedonibus in bellum civile cum ceteris superioris Asiæ populis, Eumenem secuti sunt; quo victo ad Antigonum transiere. Post hunc a Nicatore Seleuco, ac mox ab Antiocho et successoribus eius possessi: a cuius pronepote Seleuco primum defecere, primo Punico bello, L. Manlio Vulsone, M. Attilio Regulo Consulibus. . . . Eodem tempore Theodotus, mille urbium Bactrianarum præfectus, defecit, regemque se appellari jussit; quod exemplum secuti totius Orientis populi a Macedonibus defecere.—(XLI. iv.).

(c) Eodem ferme tempore, sicut in Parthis Mithridates, ita in Bactris Eucratides, magni uterque viri regna ineunt. Sed Parthorum fortuna felicior ad summum, hoc duce, imperii fastigium eos perduxit. Bactriani autem per varia bella jactati non regnum tantum, verum etiam libertatem amiserunt: siquidem Sogdianorum et Drangianorum Indorumque bellis fatigati, ad postremum ab invalidioribus Parthis, velut exsangues, oppressi sunt. Multa tamen Eucratides bella magna virtute gessit, quibus attritus, cum obsidionem Demetrii, regis Indorum, pateretur, cum CCC. militibus, LX. millia hostium assiduis eruptionibus vicit. Quinto itaque mense liberatus, Indiam in potestatem redegit. Unde cum se reciperet, a filio quem socium regni fecerat, interficitur : qui, non dissimulato parricidio, velut hostem non patrem interfecisset, et per sanguinem eius currum egit, et corpus abici insepultum iussit. Dum hæc apud Bactros geruntur, interim inter Parthos et Medos bellum oritur.—(XLI. iv.)

(d) (Seleucus) principio Babylona cepit, inde, auctis ex victoria rebus, Bactrianos expugnavit.—(XV. iv.)

II. STRABO.

(a) Νεωτρισθέντων δὲ τῶν ἔξω τοῦ Ταύρου διὰ τὸ πρὸς ἄλλοις¹ εἶναι τοὺς τῆς Συρίας καὶ τῆς Μηδίας βασιλέας, τοὺς ἔχοντας καὶ ταῦτα, πρῶτον μὲν ἀπέστησαν οἱ πεπιστευμένοι τὴν Βακτριανὴν, καὶ τὴν ἐγγὺς αὐτῆς πᾶσαν οἱ περὶ Εὐθύδημον. . . . Ἀφείλοντο δὲ (οἱ Παρθυαῖοι) καὶ τῆς Βακτριανῆς μέρος βιασάμενοι τοὺς Σκύθας, καὶ ἔτι πρότερον τοὺς περὶ Εὐκρατίδαν.

(b) οἱ δὲ Βακτριανὸν λέγουσιν αὐτὸν (Arsaces), φεύγοντα δὲ τὴν αὔξησιν τῶν περὶ Διόδοτον, ἀποστῆσαι τὴν Παρθυαίαν. (Geog., XI. ix., §§ 2-3.)

(c) Τῆς δὲ Βακτρίας μέρη μέν τινα τῇ Ἀρίᾳ παραβέβληται πρὸς ἄρκτον τὰ πολλὰ δ' ὑπέρκειται πρὸς ἕω· πολλὴ δ' ἐστὶ καὶ πάμφορος πλὴν ἐλαίου. Τοσοῦτον δὲ ἴσχυσαν οἱ ἀποστήσαντες Ἕλληνες αὐτὴν διὰ τὴν ἀρετὴν τῆς χώρας, ὥστε τῆς

¹ MSS. πρὸς ἀλλήλους.

Αριανῆς ἐπεκράτησαν, καὶ τῶν Ἰνδῶν, ὥς φησιν Ἀπολλόδωρος ὁ Ἀρταμιτηνὸς, καὶ πλείω ἔθνη κατεστρέψαντο ἢ Ἀλέξανδρος, καὶ μάλιστα Μένανδρος· εἴγε καὶ τὸν Ὕπασιν[1] διέβη πρὸς ἕω, καὶ μέχρι τοῦ Σοάνου[2] προῆλθε· τὰ μὲν γὰρ αὐτὸς, τὰ δὲ Δημήτριος ὁ Εὐθυδήμου υἱὸς τοῦ Βακτρίων βασίλεως, οὐ μόνον δὲ τὴν Πατταληνὴν κατέσχον, ἀλλὰ καὶ τῆς ἄλλης παραλίας τήν τε Σαραόστου[3] καλουμένην, καὶ τὴν Σιγέρτιδος βασιλείαν. Καθ᾽ ὅλου δέ φησιν ἐκεῖνος, τῆς συμπάσης Αριανῆς πρόσχημα εἶναι τὴν Βακτριανήν. Καὶ δὴ καὶ μέχρι Σηρῶν καὶ Φρύνων ἐξέτειναν τὴν ἀρχήν.

(d) Πόλεις δ᾽ εἶχον τά τε Βάκτρα ἥνπερ καὶ Ζαριάσπαν, ἣν διαρρεῖ ὁμώνυμος πόταμος ἐμβάλλων εἰς τὸν Ὄξον, καὶ Δάραψαν καὶ ἄλλας πλείους. Τούτων δ᾽ ἦν καὶ ἡ Εὐκρατιδιά τοῦ ἄρξαντος ἐπώνυμος. Οἱ δὲ κατασχόντες αὐτὴν Ἕλληνες καὶ ἐς σατραπείας δεῃρήκκασιν, ὧν τήν τε Ἀσπιώνου καὶ τὴν Τουριούαν ἀφῄρηντο Εὐκρατίδην οἱ Παρθυαῖοι. Ἔσχον δὲ καὶ τὴν Σογδιανὴν ὑπερκειμένην πρὸς ἕω τῆς Βακτριανῆς. . . .

(e) Τὸ μὲν οὖν παλαιὸν οὐ πολὺ διέφερον τοῖς βίοις καὶ τοῖς ἤθεσι τῶν Νομάδων οἵ τε Σογδιανοὶ καὶ οἱ Βακτριανοί. μικρὸν δ᾽ ὅμως ἡμερώτερα ἦν τὰ τῶν Βακτριανῶν· ἀλλὰ καὶ περὶ τούτων οὐ τὰ βέλτιστα λέγουσιν οἱ περὶ Ὀνησίκριτον· τοὺς γὰρ ἀπειρηκότας διὰ νόσον ἢ γῆρας, παραβάλλεσθαι τρεφομένοις κυσὶν, ἐπίτηδες δὲ πρὸς τοῦτο, οὓς " Ἐνταφιαστὰς" καλεῖσθαι τῇ πατρῴα γλώττῃ· καὶ ὁρᾶσθαι τὰ μὲν ἔξω τείχους τῆς μητροπόλεως τῶν Βάκτρων καθαρά· τῶν δ᾽ ἐντὸς τὸ πλέον ὀστέων πλῆρες ἀνθρωπίνων· καταλῦσαι δὲ τὸν νόμον Ἀλέξανδρον. Τοιαῦτα δέ πως καὶ τὰ περὶ τοὺς Κασπίους ἱστοροῦσι· τοὺς γὰρ γονέας ἐπειδὰν ἑβδομήκοντα ἔτη γεγονότες τυγχάνωσιν ἐγκλεισθέντες λιμοκτονεῖσθαι. Τοῦτο μὲν οὖν ἀνεκτότερον καὶ τῷ οἰκείῳ νόμῳ παραπλήσιον καίπερ ὂν Σκυθικὸν· πολὺ μέν τοι Σκυθικώτερον τὸ τῶν Βακτριανῶν.

(f) Φασὶ δ᾽ οὖν ὀκτὼ πόλεις τὸν Ἀλέξανδρον ἔν τε τῃ

[1] MSS. Ὕπανιν . . . Ἰσάμου.
[3] MSS. Τεσσαριόστου.

Βακτριανῇ καὶ τῇ Σογδιανῇ κτίσαι, τινὰς δὲ κατασκάψαι ὧν
Καριατας μὲν τῆς Βακτριανῆς, ἐν ᾗ Καλλισθένης συνελήφθη
καὶ παρεδόθη φυλακῇ, Μαρακάνδα δὲ τῆς Σογδιανῆς καὶ τὰ
Κύρα ἔσχατον ὃν Κύρου κτίσμα ἐπὶ τῷ Ἰαξάρτῃ ποταμῷ
κείμενον, ὅπερ ἦν ὅριον τῆς Περσῶν ἀρχῆς· κατασκαψαι δὲ τὸ
κτίσμα τοῦτο, καίπερ ὄντα φιλόκυρον, διὰ τὰς πυκνὰς ἀποσ-
τάσεις· ἑλεῖν δὲ καὶ πετρὰς ἐρυμνὰς σφόδρα ἐκ προδόσεως, τήν
τε ἐν τῇ Βακτριανῇ τὴν Σισιμίθρου ἐν ᾗ εἶχεν Ὀξυάρτης τὴν
θυγατέρα Ῥωξάνην, καὶ τὴν ἐν τῇ Σογδιανῇ καὶ τὴν τοῦ
Ὤξου, οἱ δὲ Ἀριαβάζου φασί. Τὴν μὲν οὖν Σισιμίθρου πεντε-
καίδεκα σταδίων ἱστοροῦσι τὸ ὕψος ὀγδοήκοντα δὲ τὸν κύκλον·
ἄνω δὲ ἐπίπεδον καὶ εὔγεων, ὅσον πεντακοσίους ἄνδρας τρέφειν
δυναμένην, ἐν ᾗ καὶ ξενίας τυχεῖν πολυτελοῦς καὶ γάμους
ἀγαγεῖν Ῥωξάνης τῆς Ὀξυάρτου θυγατρὸς τὸν Ἀλέξανδρον.
Τὴν δὲ τῆς Σογδιανῆς διπλασίαν τὸ ὕφος φασί. Περὶ τούτους
δὲ τοὺς τόπους καὶ τὸ τῶν Βραγχιδῶν ἄστυ ἀνελεῖν.

(g) Τὸν δὲ διὰ τῆς Σογδιανῆς ῥέοντα ποταμὸν ἐκπίπτειν εἰς
ἔρημον καὶ ἀμμώδη γῆν, καταπίνεσθαί τε εἰς τὴν ἄμμον, ὡς καὶ
τὸν Ἄριον τὸν δι᾽ Ἀρίων ῥέοντα (Geog., XI. xi., §§ 1-5).

III. QUINTUS CURTIUS.

(a) Bactrianæ terra multiplex et varia natura est.
Alibi multa arbor et vitis largos multosque fructus
alit ; solum pingue crebri fontes rigant ; qui mitiora
sunt, frumento conseruntur : cætera armentorum
pabulo cedunt. Magnam deinde partem ejusdem
terræ steriles arenæ tenent : squalida siccitate regio
non hominem, non frugem alit : cum vero venti a
Pontico mari spirant, quidquid sabuli in campis jacet,
converrunt. Quod ubi cumulatum est, magnorum
collium procul species est, omniaque pristini itineris
vestigia intereunt. Itaque, qui transeunt campos,

navigantium modo noctu sidera observant, ad quorum cursum iter dirigunt : et propemodum clarior est noctis umbra quam lux. Ergo interdiu invia est regio, quia nec vestigium quod sequantur inveniunt ; et nitor siderum caligine absconditur. Ceterum, si quos ille ventus, qui a mari exoritur, deprehendit, arena obruit. Sed qua mitior terra est, ingens hominum equorumque multitudo gignitur. [Itaque Bactriani equites XXX millia expleverunt.]

Ipsa Bactra, regionis eius caput, sita sunt sub monte Paropamisso. Bactrus amnis præterit mœnia: is urbi et regioni dedit nomen (*De Rebus Gestis Alexandri Magni*, VII. 4).

(*b*) Sogdiana regio maiori ex parte deserta est; octingenta fere stadia in latitudinem vastæ solitudines tenent. Ingens spatium rectæ regionis est, per quam amnis (Polytimetum vocant incolæ), fertur torrens. Eum ripæ in tenuem alveum cogunt; deinde caverna accipit, et sub terram rapit. Cursus absconditi indicium est aquæ meantis sonus; cum ipsum solum, sub quo tantus amnis flint, ne modico quidem resudet humore (*Ibid.*, VII. 10).

(*c*) Sunt autem Bactriani inter illas gentes promptissimi, horridis ingeniis, multumque a Persarum luxu abhorrentibus ; siti haud procul Scytharum gente bellicosissima, et rapto vivere assueti ; semperque in armis erant (*Ibid.*, IV. 6).

IV. Miscellaneous.

(*a*) Ἡ Βακτριανὴ χώρα πολλαῖς καὶ μεγάλαις οἰκουμένη πόλεσι μίαν μὲν εἶχεν ἐπιφανεστάτην ἐν ᾗ συνέβαινεν εἶναι τὰ βασίλεια· αὕτη δ᾽ ἐκαλεῖτο μὲν Βάκτρα μεγέθει ·δὲ καὶ τῇ κατὰ ἀκρόπολιν ὀχυρότητι πολὺ πασῶν δίεφερε (Diodorus Siculus, II. 6).

(*b*) Ἀφ᾽ οὗ μέχρι νῦν ἐν Βαρυγάζοις παλαιαὶ προχωροῦσι δράχμαι γράμμασιν Ἑλληνικοῖς ἐγκεχαραγμένοι ἐπίσημα τῶν μετ᾽ Ἀλέξανδρον βεβασιλευκότων Ἀπολλοδότου καὶ Μενάνδρου (*Periplus Maris Erythrœi*, XLVII.).

(*c*) Μενάνδρου δὲ τινός ἐν Βάκτροις ἐπιεικῶς βασιλεύσαντος εἶτ᾽ ἀποθανόντος ἐπὶ στρατοπέδον, τὴν μὲν ἄλλην ἐποιήσαντο κηδείαν κατὰ τὸ κοινὸν αἱ πόλεις· περὶ δὲ τῶν λειψάνων αὐτοῦ καταστάντες εἰς ἀγῶνα, πόλις συνέβησαν, ὥστε νειμάμενοι μέρος ἴσον τῆς τέφρας ἀπελθεῖν καὶ γενέσθαι μνημεῖα παρὰ πᾶσι τοῦ ἀνδρός (Plutarch, *Republicæ Gerendæ*, p. 821).

EUTHYDEMUS I

EUTHYDEMUS I

EUTHYDEMUS I

DEMETRIUS

EUTHYDEMUS II

ANTIMACHUS

EUCRATIDES

ANTIMACHUS

HELIOCLES

HELIOCLES

HELIOCLES

MENANDER

MENANDER

MENANDER

MENANDER

MENANDER

MENANDER

PHILOXEMUS

MENANDER

PHILOXEMUS

AZES

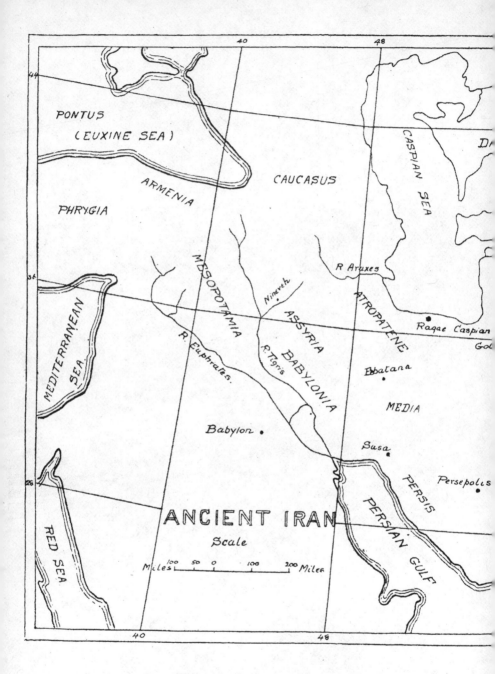

ANCIENT IRAN

Scale

Miles 100 50 0 100 200 Miles

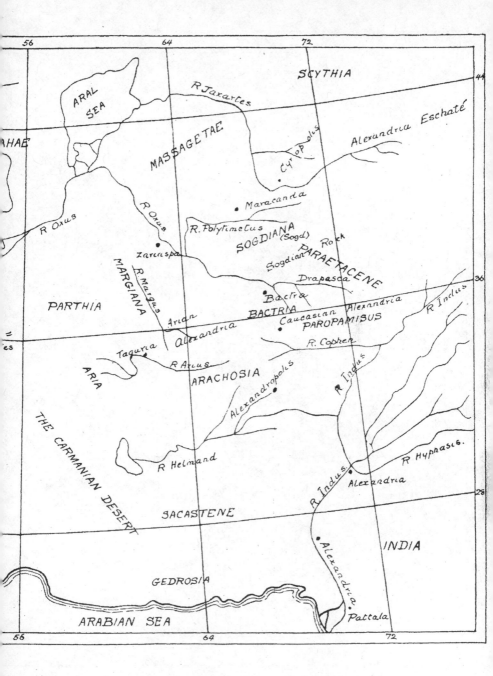

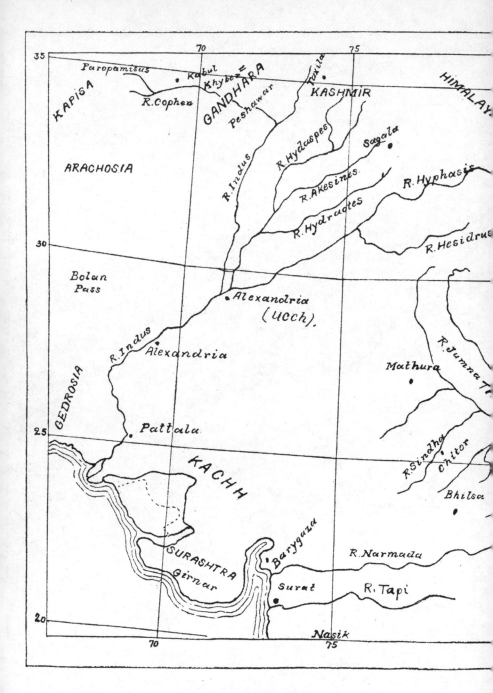

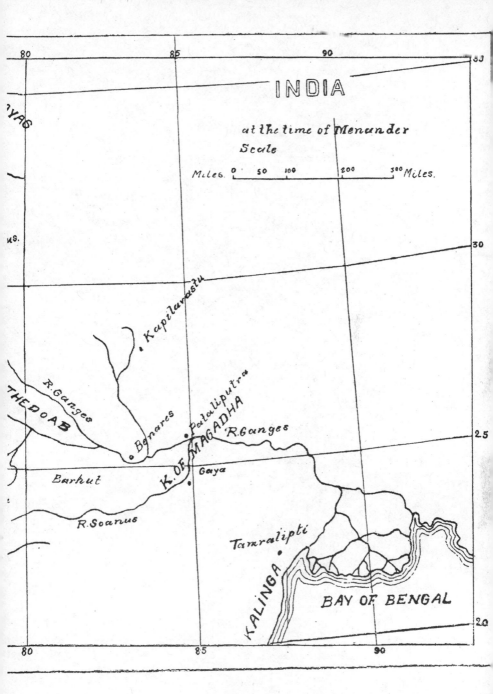

INDIA

at the time of Menander
Scale

Miles. 0 · 50 · 100 · 200 · 300 Miles.

THE DOAB

R.Ganges

Kapilavastu

Benares

Palaliputra

K. OF MAGADHA

R.Ganges

Barhut

Gaya

R.Soanus

Tamralipti

KALINGA

BAY OF BENGAL

80 · 85 · 90

30

25

20

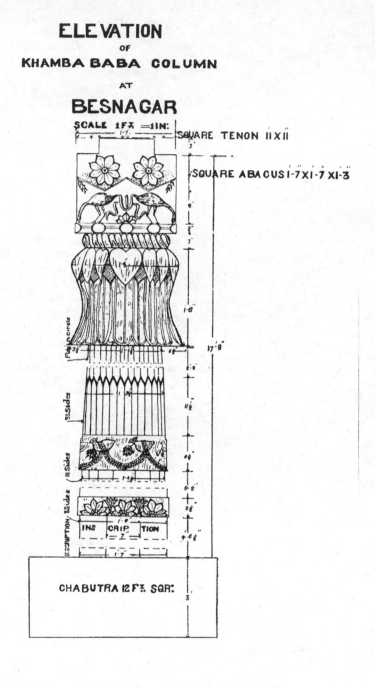

ELEVATION

OF

KHAMBA BABA COLUMN

AT

BESNAGAR

SCALE 1FT =1IN:

SQUARE TENON 11 X 11

SQUARE ABACUS 1-7 X1-7 X1-3

17'-8"

CHABUTRA 12 FT SQR:

INDEX

THE END